Soulful Sex

Weaving Sex, Love & Spirit

into Everyday Life

by Diana Owens

This book is part of the home study course
Soulful Sex: A Course of Sexual Liberation.

For more information about this course,
please visit www.lovingway.net/course

First Edition
Copyright ©2005 Diana Owens
All rights reserved.

LovingWay
Phoenix, AZ
(928) 445-7501

ISBN-13: 978-0692736814

Printed in the USA

Prologue

Dear Reader,

I remember always wanting to be good. As a little girl, that meant always doing what my parents wanted me to do. As a Catholic teenager, it meant avoiding mortal sin which would send me directly to hell, not Purgatory (the way station between heaven and hell) but pure burning fire and damnation hell! Sex, in any form, before marriage was a mortal sin. Therefore, I avoided it... no French kissing boys, and of course no petting. I refrained from "impure thoughts". I trained myself not to think about sex. I did that very well since I was deathly afraid of boys, that is until I met Jack, my husband to be. I was 17 at the time. Although I was smitten by him and very much in love, I trained myself to not have any sexual contact with him until marriage.

Why am I telling you all of this? I have come a "long

way, Baby" since those days. I became a psychotherapist and a certified sex therapist. I believe we teach what we need to learn. I definitely needed to unlearn all of the inhibitions I developed because of my Catholic upbringing and my very rigid moralistic family.

I have been interested in sacred sexuality for a very long time. During 26 years of marriage, I was interested in experiencing soulful sex. I longed to merge into my husband, into the love I felt for him and him for me, and into the light I felt was all around us when we would make love. I can count on one hand how often that happened for us.

I wish I knew then what I know now. Jack was not interested in learning about sacred sexuality. Neither were the other men I had relationships with after our marriage ended. I am now 61 and have been single for over 10 years.

Several years ago, although I was single and without a life partner or even a sex partner, I decided I would get further training in sacred sexuality. My intention was to learn enough so that I could pass onto my clients skills about how to blend sexuality, spirituality and love into their intimate sexual relationship and into their daily lives. What I didn't know was how much I would be transformed through this process.

This book tells the tale of my transformation through the workshops in sacred sexuality that I attended. It also is a culmination of my life's work as a sex therapist and a psychotherapist. I feel so blessed for all the many hours I have spent conversing with my clients, teaching them and reminding myself how to heal, how to love myself, my partner and all of life. I feel so privileged to have been invited into their lives and into the inner sanctum of their souls. I learned from each one of them and I thank them all. In this book, I share a lot of the wisdom I passed on to them and they passed on to me.

This book would not have happened without my friend Bill's inspiration and support and expertise. He convinced me I had something important to say and showed me how it could be fun and easy if we did it as a team. Bill offered me a way to write the book that I am most comfortable with which is an interview style. We simply talked to each other the way I have talked to my clients all of these years. I invite you to join our discussion. As Bill and I talk, I invite you to formulate your own questions and relate to your own experience. Join in our dialogue!

I have added homework exercises at the end of the book so that you can apply your learning to your life. Over the years, I have done this with many of my clients. I have found this is the best way to deepen learning and retain what you learn. I would love your emails to me as a way of dialoging about the concepts in the book. This book can be a mini workshop for you to learn about sacred sexuality in your own way and at your own speed. It is designed for the ordinary person who knows little or nothing about sacred sexuality or the experienced practitioner who has practiced for a long time.

You can deepen your experience of sacred sexuality wherever you are on the path. I have used the words sacred sexuality and soulful sex interchangeably because I believe when we open our souls to each other through sexuality, it is sacred. The body of knowledge on sacred sexuality in our western culture teaches people how to access their soul so they can have soulful sex regularly as a way of expressing their deep love for their partner. By the soul, I mean the principle of life, love and goodness that is in each one of us.

The format of the book is an introductory interview with Bill, my publisher and co-interviewer, as a way for you to get to know him. He then interviews me in depth as to my introduction to sacred sexuality, what drew me to it and how

I have benefited from it. Bill then interviews me to establish a foundation for the direction I'm taking in this book. I then offer my interviews of experts in the field of Sacred Sexuality as a way to deepen your understanding and experience of the various aspects of sacred sexuality.

I then offer you another discussion Bill and I have on Relationship as Spiritual Path, which is the primary way I view sacred sexuality. You are then introduced to Bill and Melanie who are married and have been together for about two years. They share their intimate practices of sacred sexuality and how it has affected their lives. We then end our discussion with an enlightened interview with Margot Anand about how another culture views sexuality and the possibilities in our culture to celebrate and venerate sacred sexuality as meaningful and relevant in all areas of our life and of our society.

Thank you for taking this soul-full journey with me. Happy travels. May we stay in touch and may you deepen your experience of loving through your reading this book and applying it to your life!

Blessings,

Diana

Forward

A man's perspective of sacred sexuality: Diana's interview with Bill, her book publisher and producer of her sacred sexuality interview series

Diana: Thank you so much for speaking with me today. Bill, you have had a lot of experience in learning about people, personal growth, and what makes people happy through your work in communications over the last 30 years—both on radio and now on the internet. So, my first question to you is, if you could give a gift—one piece of information or advice—to people all over the world that would enhance their happiness and increase their fulfillment in their personal relationships, what would that be?

Bill: Well, it's my belief, Diana, is that inside every human being is this incredible potential for ecstasy and bliss. You could say that it lives in the sex organs, but actually it lives in the heart and soul. It's a state of mind, and really, a state of being. It's an opportunity, a doorway, that all we have to do is learn about. Once we know what it is, how it's accessed, and how it's applied, our lives will never be the same. That's what happened to me.

D: The way you expressed this sounds incredible. I was thinking that ecstasy and bliss are not something that people talk about in our culture or in many other cultures in the world. So, I'm curious: how did this happen to you?

B: Well, as a young man, when I passed through puberty, I started to have orgasms—initially through personal experimentation, and later, in partnership with my girlfriend. I found that after each orgasm, I had a clarity of thinking that I had never experienced before. It was as if a lightning bolt had passed through my body and entered into my brain. This clarity gave me many insights. I even gave a name to them—I called them 'constructions'. In other words, these insights were new ways of looking at reality that were different from ordinary thinking and programmed reactivity. Now you understand that I'm just fourteen years old when this is all going on.

D: Goodness. It's like you were a natural Tantrika, and didn't even know it.

B: That's exactly what it was. I had a girlfriend at the time, and I started keeping a diary of these experiences. And, of course, this was a very private diary, though it didn't have so many details about fantasy, or what I was doing with myself, or what I was thinking about. It was mainly about the insights I was able to derive after these climaxes. And so, I started to make a practice of using orgasm as a tool. Now, very soon thereafter—and this was the time of the late sixties—psychedelic experimentation also showed me the same doorways. And I realized that sexual power, sexual energy, is actually just energy. It is actually a release of energy into the brain. Being the little scientist I was, I realized that sexual energy is just another form of energy in the body. When I started to read about it, I learned that that was actually true. So, that was kind of amazing to me, although these weren't ideas I spoke about with very many people back then. You know, when you're fourteen and fifteen years old, people aren't talking about that at all. They're thinking about, "Gee, am I going to get a kiss from this girl or not?"

D: Right. Well, that's what was interesting to me about what you say. This didn't happen just in your partnerships with girls or women. It happened through masturbation and your individual experiences with sexuality?

B: Yes, what it did for me, Diana, was to provide a context for love-making as something not just sacred and special, but life-changing. In other words, I started to get perspectives on things I hadn't seen before. After an orgasm, I would often see something that I called 'the personality'— which was something that was different from my true self. And I began to draw these little diagrams depicting this, and my high school sweet heart and I began to look at these things and talk about it. I explored it and utilized it; my sexuality was actually part of my meditation practice.

D: It was back then?

B: It was back then. I think I was seventeen when I first started going to the library and looking up information about this. That's when I heard about the Ananaga Ranga and the Kama Sutra. And, frankly, Diana, I was pretty disappointed. These books were very esoteric. They were telling me, for example, "Anoint the feet of your lover with these oils for seven days." That didn't seem to have anything to do with the transformative, raw, immediate power of one's own sexuality, of the power of the energy that can course through a human being's body.

D: Well, Bill, it sounds like there was something that happened to you besides pleasure. The pleasure was important, but the experience of clarity about yourself and about life—and also the experience of connection with your self and with life—made this, as you were saying, a cosmic and a blissful experience beyond pleasure.

B: Yes, and it actually even had political ramifications, because it made me question my own thinking and beliefs. It shook my world. My parents were a very conservative, Republican family, and when I started having these insightful experiences, I suddenly began to realize that I didn't fit within those models. I didn't relate to their worldview and values. Deep down, I was feeling the need, as Joseph Campbell later called it, to "follow my bliss". Maybe what I really needed to do was to see where an unfettered mind can go. And so I began to question everything: what my beliefs were, who I was hanging out with, what kind of people and friends I wanted to have, what was I going to do for a living.

I had originally intended to be an aero-space engineer. And then I realized, "Well, that's going to make me a good living, but maybe I don't really don't want to build cruise missiles for a living. Maybe I want to do something a little more creative. So I went into pure science, into astronomy and physics. This impacted me very deeply, very quickly. Frankly, I thought everybody was having these kind of experiences, but they were just too personal, and so they weren't talking about them. Because I considered myself to be a little junior scientist, I just decided to be a scientist about myself. I decided to do my own self-experimentation.

D: Well, how interesting, Bill, that early in your life, you were not fully aware of the nature of these experiences you were having, but still you had an integrated experience of your body, and this energy of the body opened up your mind. How beautiful that this helped you search for the answers as to what was happening to you, and why you were experiencing these very cosmic, connected, clarifying experiences that included your heart, your body, and your mind. And, certainly, it went beyond all of that: the experience of your soul.

B: I think that's very important—what you said about the heart, Diana—because I felt this tremendous opening in my chest from those experiences. I later became a devotee of Baba Ram Dass, who was formerly Richard Albert, a Harvard scientist who found a spiritual teacher in India. His path was the Bhakti path, the path of heart opening. I think that because my first sexual experiences were so heart opening, I always considered sex to be sacred. And I've only had sacred sexual experiences. I don't know about anything else. It just doesn't even interest me.

D: Well I'm curious, Bill. You equate the opening of the heart with sacred sexuality. Will you talk about what you mean when you say you experience sex as sacred because of the heart's opening?

B: Well, I was able to make a connection between the sexual energy that rose up, entered my chest and opened my heart, with the experience of a state of undefendedness and intimacy with my lover. This started in high school, and it's been my experience my whole life. I don't make love with anyone that I don't feel a close heart connection with. I've been blessed, I think, because of that, to have many, many close women friends—whether they were lovers or not. And so, I would say that I think that that's part of the gift of tantra.

It wasn't until later in my life that I became formally introduced to tantra via Margot Anand's first book. I read it and found, "Oh, here it is!" Margot was describing so beautifully and clearly some of what I had been experiencing. Because the Western approach to tantra is far more clear and specific than some of the more ancient texts, which may contain some good information, but are fairly obscure and kind of mysterious—perhaps to protect the author. Margot's book was based on her own personal experiences and what she learned. And so it had far more meaning and personal relevance to me.

D: What is your definition of 'sacred sexuality'?

B: My definition of sacred sexuality, Diana, begins with the idea that you come to it with reverence. You see it as a vehicle of transformation, and you expect your sexual experience to be transformative, you demand it for yourself. Not saying, "Oh, this is just going to be some fun, little, sweet experience." You approach sex knowing that great pleasure, ecstasy, and bliss are there waiting for you. And, as we know, if your expectation and direction and intentions are there, there's a greater chance for that to happen.

D: Are you talking only about the sexual experiences that you have?

B: No. I could apply this to any kind of spiritual practice. As you know, I've been a Sufi for over thirty-five years, and that's called "The Path of the Broken Heart"— meaning that all of us have broken hearts in some way, and the Sufi path helps us to reopen the heart. I'm also a student of the Diamond Approach, which you and I share, and that's a very heart-centered practice as well. So it's not just sexuality where we can experience transformation, but it is inclusive to that. Certainly you can touch God without an orgasm. But, if you don't expect—in your sexual experiences; in your repertoire of erotic contact—if you don't expect God to be there, then I think you're cutting yourself very short.

And I feel like that's bringing us to this whole discussion of why you and I are doing this book.

D: Which is...? I'm curious to hear, in your words.

B: Well, I believe that the message of the book, Diana, is that we all can live and love in a bold, clear, passionate way. This is a valid and beautiful path of liberation. Certainly there are many writers and teachers—David Deida, Margot Anand, Steve and Lokita Carter—who are talking about this. But I don't know of any book that, through a series of interviews with experts in the field and my interviews with you, where sacred sexuality is actually explored personally, completely, directly, and without hesitation.

D: Well it's interesting, Bill, it's as though this is a culmination for you of what started earlier in your life as a seed, an energy seed, that began transforming your own experience, your own way of living. And it sounds like over the years you've really sought answers as to why you had this experience. You later found tantra, and you've read many books on it. What does the book that you and I are creating offer to others that isn't found in other books on sacred sexuality, tantra, love, sexuality, or spirituality?

B: What our book does is look into, almost with a scientist-like inquiry, the basic nature of these forces of sexuality, love, and spirituality. And it's done in an interview style. I'm interviewing you, you're interviewing other teachers of tantra. Between your expertise, Diana, and the expertise of the teachers, this information is revealed in a story that no one else has told. And that story is the story of your sexual liberation and transformation through tantra.

D: Yes, Bill. And yours!

B: Absolutely. We form the male and female counterparts; the male and female aspects, having a long, rich, and varied conversation that is an adventure of discovery and insight. The entire book is written in the form of a dialogue, which is a more relaxed, informal, and intimate means of communicating the mysteries of sacred sexuality. They're communicated in this book, I think, in a very accessible and enjoyable style.

D: So do tell me about the choice of the interview style as a way of communicating this message to people.

B: Well, the interview style has a spontaneity and an immediacy to it. We actually recorded these interviews live and later edited them for print. In the editing, we kept the conversational style, so that it maintains the feeling of two people sitting together with tea and talking. In your conversations with me, you have an opportunity to tell your story, which is filled with the learnings you've gained over the years through your work and your personal experiences. In your conversations with tantra teachers—Margot Anand, Steve and Lokita Carter, Gaia Reblitz—there is the opportunity to hear some of their personal stories, and in that, partake in their incredible understanding and wisdom.

D: When did you get the idea for this book?

B: Long before the book idea began to emerge, you and I had recorded these interviews initially as educational audio CDs. You interviewed Margot, Steve and Lokita, then I interviewed you in commentaries on those interviews. These recordings were so popular, it occurred to me one day that a compilation of these conversations into book form would be fantastic. The name of the book emerged shortly thereafter.

Truthfully, I've been wanting to be involved in a project like this for twenty-five or thirty years. I wanted to bring light to the very misunderstood area of tantra, love, sexuality and spirituality, and to bring some of my own perspectives to it as well. I also wanted someone to work with who knew a lot about it and had a similar attitude, especially since there is so much emotional charge and misunderstanding around sexuality. Sacred sexuality is simply harnessing the natural procreative and transformative forces in our body. Unfortunately, there's a great deal of confusion among people about this.

What I've found in our conversations, Diana, in the retreats and workshops we've attended in common, and as I got to know you as a friend, is that you share this same vision about educating the public about sacred sexuality, love and intimacy. That's wonderful, but that in and of itself doesn't necessarily make you a great teacher. What makes you a great teacher, Diana, is that you are comfortable with this vision, and you are comfortable with talking about the most intimate—perhaps even painful—parts of it, just as I am. Here you are interviewing me about the book, trying to give our readers a little sense of who the interviewer is, and I'm already talking about masturbation in the first question, you know? If I had hang-ups about that, you would never have heard the story. And you and the reader would never know that my early personal experiences of transformative sexual energy was a core motivator for me to do this book.

So I have found, over the years of knowing you and doing interviews with you, that you and I flow through the way that we can go right to the nut of it, right to the kernel of something, without hesitation, without hiding, without being smart alecks about it. Working with you in creating these recordings was a dream come true for me. Putting these conversations into a book was a natural outflow of this. And I just had to do it with you.

D: That's wonderful, Bill. I think there's something in the book for everyone, because we certainly have encompassed many aspects of Sacred Sexuality, both from a very educational standpoint, as in the interviews with Margot, which are filled with wisdom, as well as from personal experience in the stories told by you or me or Lokita Carter or Gaia Reblitz.

Story is such a potent conveyor of high teachings. You talk about your early sexual experiences, your masturbation and early love-making with females, which drew you into experiences that became cosmic for you. But you didn't know it was going to be cosmic. It was because of your interest in pleasure and the connection, the love that you felt, or the attraction you felt for a woman back then. Over the years, you were drawn into this experience and later discovered that this energy is much more than pleasure in the body. You tapped into the remarkable, wondrous realms of sacred sexuality that most people don't even hear about, let alone experience. Your story about this personal discovery of tantra and transformative sexual energy can be a teaching, a source of insight, for others.

I do believe that people can learn something on all levels. There are exercises in the book that have to do with enhancing the pleasure of the physical act of love-making, whether with a partner or in the act of love-making to oneself, masturbation. Then we will look at, "So what else is there, beyond the pleasure and the physical act?" This will bring forth into our sexuality the connection with the heart, the opening of the mind, and the cosmic connection with all of life. These facets of sexuality are something that people may not be so familiar with or clear about. It seems to me that you and I have lived that, we didn't just learn it from a book, but we've lived it. I feel tremendously grateful for this approach, for the words that can name it, for the pathways that develop these practices and expand these experiences of sacred sexuality.

B: My first lover became my first wife. And, in the

beginning, I learned how to please her mainly by asking her what felt good. But what I saw—when she would go through an orgasmic or a multi-orgasmic experience—is that she was changed. Not just changed psychologically, but changed as a person. And so I started to become interested, as her lover, in what it was that was changing her. As this became a focus, our love-making stopped being so much about giving her the perfect pleasure. It was more about bringing about and supporting the change that came out of the pleasure.

This is something that you and I completely understand, Diana, from personal experience, which made it possible for you and I to have this dialogue in a completely open, undefended way. I think that's what makes this book valuable: that we're going into this in a dialogue fashion, searching for the truth of it, and we really don't care what we have to expose, what we have to look at to get there—whether it's our own hang-ups, whether it's very private, personal feelings and information, or whether it's a vision for life that maybe some of our friends would think is just too outrageous.

D: You talk about the undefendedness that happens—the openness that happens—when this energy gets triggered and then is both expressed and enhanced. I think the openness doesn't have to just come through orgasm. I remember an experience of my own during a tantra workshop that I was participating in where there had been a lot of work where people were opening up, because of some of the exercises that we had done. When we gathered in a circle at the end of the exercises, a lot of people were nude because they had been participating in exercises of touching each other and enhancing the energy through touching. In the workshop overall, not everyone was nude because each person had the prerogative of how much they would undress.

And so, here we are in this circle, some nude, some dressed, and each person was then very spontaneously invited to come into the center of the circle and dance. Each person danced their dance, and the others started uninhibitedly clapping and cheering for them. And it was so wonderful to see each person expressing in such a passionate, uninhibited, spontaneous, open, and free way—their exuberance of being free, and loving, and feeling good about themselves, their body, and their experience.

This was a culmination of the work that people had been doing individually and as couples. At the end of our dance experience—and everyone was so high—the leader of the group said, "This is what tantra is about: the transformation of life, one person at a time." We heard this and there was a glow emanating from everyone in the group in agreement, because we all felt this transformation that was entirely based on openness. I can still feel that experience, I can still feel the connection with others through all the energy that was there. I know people took that back into their personal relationship with themselves and with others, and were actually changed, just like you said. So it's not just orgasm that can be freeing and transformative, it's the opening of the heart that occurs when people open up with their bodies and with their minds.

B: I think that our readers, Diana, will not only feel themselves change as they join us in this dialogue—in this adventure into bliss and understanding—but I think they're also going to see you and I mature as we write the book. In other words, as we work together, digesting this information, learning from some of the great tantric teachers who you've interviewed, they'll also watch us be transformed further. And so this dialogue method is a way for the reader to directly participate. And, certainly, if they're interested, they can go further—working with the tapes and the practices, and working with you directly—and make it a life-changing curriculum of transformation.

D: Well I'm curious, Bill. You have a very intense history of working in the field of communication. So I think you speak from a large amount of expertise, talent and experience you've had with all kinds of people. Would you please tell our readers how you got into this field, what kind of work you do, and how does this book project compare to some of the other things that you've done?

B: Well, in my early twenties, I wanted to fund some very expensive astronomical research. I was told that I would just have to become a tenured professor, and that was going to be that. But I realized that a lot of money could be made in the entertainment and communications industry, which was another area where I had a lot of strength and experience at the time. And so I started working in radio and television at a very early age, mostly in public radio and public TV. I had an opportunity to interview all kinds of people: scientists, researchers, teachers, thinkers—folks like Stuart Wilde, Andrew Harvey, Deepak Chopra, Neil Donald Walsh, James Redfield. I had all these various shows, and I was involved as an interviewer, producer, and editor.

Gradually, I started to see myself as someone who could get information out of people in a way that really made it easy for others to understand. And so, here you come along, Diana, with all of your experience—as a sex therapist, a psychotherapist, a yoga teacher, a tantra practitioner, a student of the Diamond Approach. You and I share this wonderful form of spiritual practice that includes a form of Socratic inquiry along with meditation—something that puts together depth psychology with spirituality.

Our enormous background of relatedness made you the

ideal person for me to fulfill this dream of exploring tantra in a public way—in a way through which others could learn from it. So, what a beautiful opportunity and what a privilege it has been for me, Diana, to work with you to refine and hone this message. As two tantric practitioners, it is a phenomenal experience to sit back and share what we have discovered, to respond to what we have learned, and to comment on what has been revealed in your interviews with these tantra masters. And so, what the reader is going to experience—whether they take your course work or not; even if they just read the book—is a progression and a change in you, in me, and in themselves. This is one of my dreams come true. This is what I've told you from the beginning, and why I'm so excited about this project. It's a story that needs to be told. And I believe it needs to be told in this way.

D: Well, I feel grateful and very appreciative of my friendship with you, Bill. We have been friends for about ten years, now. And, as you say, our common bond has been in the spiritual seeking that we've done, through the Diamond Heart work and the Sufi work. Then, I remember, several years ago, when I was telling you about my interest and my training in tantra, you had the idea of inviting me to be interviewed by you on a program you were doing. We then discovered our interest in internet and how we offer interesting educational material through the internet. And now we're doing this work on the book together. It all has evolved so beautifully.

I feel like our coming together has been a part of our spiritual practice. I do believe there are no accidents. Our passion for growing and for transformation through sexuality, spirituality, and love have been something that we both share, and we both are very committed to teaching others about, I feel extremely grateful for this time of talking with you and hearing the rich, amazing background that you have, that has led you to this point. I feel excited about the interviews—that you have done of me and that I've done with others. And now, the cycle is complete, with my opportunity to interview you.

B: Well, what a treat. I would add one more thing, Diana. These conversations that are now in this book actually began when you and I were at these spiritual retreats together, and we would start sharing our experiences. It was in that moment that I had the idea of interviewing you and putting you on a radio show in Santa Fe. We had no idea then what that would lead to; here we are, finishing a book.

I want to say that, if I had the opportunity to eavesdrop on our conversation, I would be thrilled. Everyone who reads this book will get a chance to participate—at least vicariously—in this exploration. They will also have a chance to get to know you, Diana, and hear your story as a Tantrika in transformation. You are such a mature woman, with a lifetime of experience and a tremendous ability to guide others in their transformative process.

D: Well, thank you, Bill. I think you have a wonderful gift of highlighting and spotlighting people's grace and ability. I feel very grateful about how you've done that for me, and with me, and with the people that I've interviewed. So I thank you for being an enlightened being yourself, and bringing light to my life—and to all those who I've had the privilege to interview for this book.

Chapter 1:

Discovering Sacred Sexuality

In this conversation about her discovery and early experiences of tantra, Diana illuminates the fundamental essence of soulful sex and how it can enhance lovemaking in a person or couple's everyday life.

Bill: I am honored and delighted to be working with you, Diana, on this fascinating and invaluable topic. I agree with Margot Anand that tantra is a potent and very whole-person path of awakening. Let's begin by defining 'tantra'; what is the meaning and metaphor of this ancient word?

Diana: I want to be very clear from the beginning that my approach to tantra by no means incorporates the great body of knowledge of tantra yoga that is vast, complex and ancient. Tantra yoga originated in India around the fourteenth century. It is very deep and would take years to master.

I have studied with Margot Anand who has adapted principles of tantra yoga and blended them with western psychology, philosophy and spirituality. The primary focus of Margot's approach is that liberation includes the body and that everything in life is accepted as part of the divine whole.

The fundamental meaning of tantra is 'to weave.' What this means is that those who study tantra learn to weave the whole of everything into life and into their practices. They learn to integrate love, sex, and spirituality into the fabric of their life. They aim to not limit or exclude any part of life in their spiritual practice.

B: So it's a living practice.

D: It's a living practice, and it's an integrated spiritual path that is inclusive of a person's entire life experience.

B: So, it's really not a matter of doing tantra one hour a day or five hours a week, as one does in a sitting meditation practice. It's more of an integrated practice, like certain forms of yoga, such as karma yoga or being a householder in the Buddhist tradition, where every act of your life is some expression of the spiritual path.

D: Exactly. What I like and what I've found personally helpful in my own spiritual practice is the work with energy. The ancient tantra practitioners, who practiced meditation and committed to living a life of deep holiness and spirituality, recognized that the energy of sexuality is powerful. It can be used to heighten our experience of the heart opening in love to ourselves and to the people in our lives who are important to us. In Tantric practice we bring the energy of survival and sexuality that's very powerful in the first and second chakras up to the heart chakra, the center of love. We then bring this heart energy up to the brain and the 6th and 7th chakras which are the centers of intuition and connection with the divine. This allows the energies of loving and connecting to the divine to be strengthened and intensified, so that we can use them more fully in practicing life as loving and present. (See diagrams on pages 201 and 202.)

B: That's fascinating, Diana.

D: I've really become so appreciative and respectful of this tantra way of living. It is much more than getting sexually turned on or high. It's really about moving energy for loving and for ecstatic ways of living as well.

B: I like this idea. If you're taking the survival instinct and the procreative forces in the body, which are biological imperatives, and you're raising them into these higher centers, that's an incredibly powerful experience all by itself.

D: Yes, it is.

B: And it's as though working with these energies in this way has a purifying effect; that the tantra practitioner can have a purification experience in their practice.

D: Yes, I agree. I think we're all attracted to living our relationships in as loving, positive, harmonious, and ecstatic ways as we can. And so, I think the draw of tantra is that it integrates the energy of survival and procreation—as you talked about—which are very strong energies, into the energy of loving and connecting with all of life. Most all of us want to improve our ability to love and to resolve the blocks within us that keep us from loving in the most open and generous ways as we can.

Tantra also addresses those blocks of the ego that keep us from living in loving, open, happy, and caring ways. So— and I love this part, Bill—tantra gives one the hope of ecstasy. I haven't said the word 'ecstasy' as much in my life as I've said it since I've started to study tantra. And how wonderful that we can have the hope and the possibility, and then the practical skill-building techniques, to live ecstatically! Wouldn't you agree?

B: Oh, absolutely. Now, I know that Margot Anand has been a primary teacher to you, and many years ago she developed the SkyDancing School. Would you tell us a little about that?

D: Well, SkyDancing is the school of tantra that Margo Anand developed over twenty years ago, through the study that she did of tantra. And what she learned is that tantra itself is a very intense and complex body of teaching that is ancient. Much of tantra includes rituals and traditions and theory that is not relevant or particularly helpful to the Western culture and the citizens of our particular nation.

B: Are you referring to texts like the Kama Sutra and the Ananga Ranga? I've looked at those, Diana, they're very confusing. I can't follow that material at all.

D: [Laughter] Exactly. She developed the School of SkyDancing tantra based on an enlightened female Buddha who lived in eighth century Tibet. She has been called the SkyDancer, which is a metaphor for dancing in the sky in celebration of her ecstatic state. Margot has extracted the essence of these esoteric teachings and brought it to Westerners in a language they can understand and apply meaningfully in their lives. So SkyDancing is really an integration of tantra principles, rituals, and practices, along with Western psychology—transpersonal psychology, sexology, yoga, music, modern techniques of bioenergetics, neurolinguistic programming, visualization, communication skills, and most importantly the energy map of the chakras.

So the emphasis in SkyDancing tantra is to open the heart and to create ecstatic living—to actually achieve ecstatic states. SkyDancing refers to the ability to achieve ecstatic states. Margot's SkyDancing tantra integrates these ecstatic states into our sexuality, so that love can be experienced as a flow, a joyful celebration, and a healing meditation.

B: What you're saying, then, is that Margot's SkyDancing School actually incorporates some of the more modern psychology technologies and some of the more recent information that we have about sexual ecstasy.

D: Right. So I think it's a very helpful way that Westerners can implement very complex and perhaps difficult concepts into a practice and a perspective that is useful, effective, and that actually allows them to heighten their own experience of ecstasy and intimacy with themselves, all of life, and if they have a partner, with that particular person in their lives.

B: I'm curious, Diana, how did you first get introduced to tantra? What is this process of transformation that you went through, from a wife and mother, to psychotherapist, to a tantrika?

D: Well, there are two parts to the answer to this question, Bill, because the introduction to tantra came much later in my life than the interest. I couldn't have articulated what I was looking for in my relationship with my husband, but I knew that sex, in and of itself, wasn't as complete or as fulfilling as I would have liked it to be. He and I were very in love, and very connected to each other on every level, for a long time. And yet I would go away from our lovemaking with a sense of not being able to express all the love that was inside of me. So there was a sense of emptiness, a sense of frustration at times, a sense that there could be more.

Even though I often felt close to my husband during sex, it was as though sex wasn't the container I was looking for to express all of the love that I felt, all of the connection. And what I know now about that—because now I can articulate it—is that it was a soul connection I yearned to share. It was the life force in both of us that I sought to connect with. My husband and I wanted a way, and needed a way, to connect to each other, and to express ourselves in this way. And so, I would say, from the very beginning of my relationship with my husband—we got married when I was 22—and from that point on, until I got divorced when I was 48, I was very interested in finding ways of expressing our love, and the deep sense of closeness and unity we felt.

I had sex for the first time when I got married. Being a good Catholic girl, I followed the Catholic Church's direction about that. The Catholic Church taught that sex before marriage is a mortal sin. And so, of course I wasn't going to do that.

B: Well, that's pretty interesting. Your initial introduction to sex was with your husband; you had had no sexual partners prior to getting married.

D: No sexual partners at all, and no expression of sexuality at all—except kissing. [Laughter] I would kiss the boys that I was attracted to in high school. I met my husband when I was 17, and we dated for 5 years before marriage, but because the Catholic Church had—I'm going to use the term, 'brain washed' me—and because, in the name of my wanting to be a good person and live a good, loving, and responsible life, I followed the Catholic Church's direction to the letter of the law—not wanting to do anything that would take away my goodness. And the Catholic Church taught us that sex, even thoughts about sex, thoughts or any actions, or any desires, were a mortal sin. A mortal sin means that you could go to hell if you thought thoughts about sexuality, or if you behaved sexually in any way. I remember a book we were reading in high school that was on the Church's X-rated list. It was called Peyton Place, and it was being passed around our class. I would not read it, because I knew I would commit a mortal sin if I read anything that was sexy or sexual. So my Catholic upbringing was that strict.

B: And they later turned Peyton Place into a television program.

D: Right. So now everybody gets to see it, but I couldn't even think about it or read about it, because that was a mortal sin. Knowing what I know now, I actually call this spiritual rape. Rape is a very strong word, but what I mean by that is that the Catholic Church, and my interpretation of the Catholic Church, took my desire to be a good person, and perverted it. I think the Church really took advantage of my desire to be good, and caused me to repress my energy—the life force within me around sexuality—until it was actually non-existent.

So I met my husband when I was 17, and he and I were deeply in love from the very beginning of our relationship. For 5 years we dated, and during that time we didn't have any kind of sexual contact, except regular kissing—no French kissing, no caressing of any areas of the body below the neck and the above the knees.

B: Oh, my goodness. And during that time you really believed that if you had sexual thoughts about your fiancé, that this would be harmful to you?

D: That it would be spiritually negative. That it was evil. The Catholic Church taught me it was evil.

B: Wow.

D: Again, what I know now is that my soul was longing to express its goodness, and to experience the goodness of who I am. And I now know that the essence of all of us is good. So I've found ways, more and more, to experience and express my goodness. Tantra has become one of those ways. It is a vehicle that could express my life force, as well as my soul. What I call my soul is my life force, and the center, the source of my aliveness, the source of my capacity to love. I've really felt excited and grateful to have discovered this beautiful path of tantra that opens the heart as well as the energies in the body.

I have come to understand that our life force needs to be supported, and that the body is a vehicle of the soul. The body is as sacred as any other ways of expressing love are. But I didn't know that earlier in my life, because of the Church's influence. It's a cultural phenomenon, and also religious, that many religions and churches in the Western culture have split the body and the soul in half. The body is split off as evil, as a source of negativity, and it will pull us down spiritually. And then it is taught that spirituality, our soul, is supposed to be connected to God, the sky, to good works and good deeds that don't include the body. From the Western culture's perspective and the spiritual religious perspective of the Western churches, the body takes away from our goodness. That is not what I now believe, and it's certainly not what tantrists' believe.

B: Well, what an amazing belief system to work through. How did you do it? How did you get from there to where you are now, as a tantrika?

D: As a sex therapist, I've learned that the two major influences that define our sexuality and our belief system: the church and the family. My own family was an extremely great source of repression in my life. My father became a Catholic because, in his family, there were many divorces, and the Catholic Church made divorce a mortal sin. He wanted as many controls as possible against getting a divorce. So he became a Catholic to prevent his own marriage from ending in divorce. But he was extremely repressed sexually.

He was so angry about sex, and so determined to control sex in my sisters—he was adamant that there not be any kind of sexual expression before marriage—that with two of my sisters, he actually—and I'll use the term—'bush whacked' them. In one of these incidents, one of my sisters was out on the golf course making out with her boyfriend, and my father followed her, snuck up on her and her boyfriend, and dragged her home, yelling at her and telling her boyfriend to leave. He shamed both of them and embarrassed her totally. In a similar situation, my other sister was making out in front of her boyfriend's house. They were in the car, and my father went over and, again, dragged her out of the car and yelled at her, telling her she was horrible and a slut.

This was the kind of background that I had, and when I was preparing for marriage, I went to the doctor for a premarital exam. The doctor was simply checking my breasts and checking my vagina, and the minute he put his hands on me, I had this emotional outburst. I just burst into tears, because I had had this image of saving myself totally for the man that I was going to marry. I felt a sense of violation and tragedy, that this was a terrible, awful thing that had happened. In that incident, all of this repression that I'd had in my growing up years came out.

I'm telling this story because, as a sex therapist, I know that I'm not the only one who has wounds in the area of sexuality. Also, I believe I have wounds in the area of spirituality, because, in the name of my desire for goodness, I repressed my sexuality totally. People who have had similar backgrounds, in their family life, in their church, or in their life experiences, have, in the name of their desire for goodness, done the same thing. And it ends up distorting the experience of sexuality. Sexuality becomes somehow wrong or harmful.

B: So here you are, you're in a long marriage, beginning to feel a frustration with your sexual connection. What then brought you to tantra? How did you discover it and how did you get there?

D: Actually, I asked my husband to go to tantra workshops many times in our marriage, and he didn't, he wouldn't, he wasn't interested. He was content with things the way they were, so we never went together to a tantra workshop. We were married 26 years, and it was toward the end of our marriage that I was really looking very actively for something that would help bridge the distance that I felt between us. And because he wasn't interested, he wouldn't look beyond the place where we were. So we ended up getting a divorce. I've been single for 10 years now.

During the time I was single, I asked several of my partners if they would go to a tantra workshop, and they too were not interested. Then one man went to a workshop with me, a weekend workshop, which is where I first met Margot Anand, who became my primary teacher. But he chose not to continue. He didn't think it was anything special. I was still very attracted to it, but at the time I was more interested in spending time with my partner than I was in growth experiences. So I settled, I gave in. I didn't follow my heart, which had been interested in tantra for a long time. So it's only been in the last two years that I decided that I was going to pursue tantra, with a partner or not. It's kind of like what happens when we all mature. I feel that this is a maturing process for me, that I'm not going to wait for a man to do the things that I really want to do.

I know now that tantra is the integration of spirituality

and sexuality. It's both permission-giving, as well as an experience that heightens and integrates sexual energy with spiritual energy. And when I say spiritual energy, I mean the life force within us, the sense of ability to love, the energy that's about loving, that's about joy, that's about aliveness and presence. The life force is the experience of who I am, and the unique expression of who I am as a human being and as a spiritual being. This is what spirituality means to me. Learning to integrate the energy of sexuality and the energy of spirituality is what I had been looking for. And so I actively sought out teachers who I thought had the same values that I did.

B: I just think it's amazing, Diana, that Margot Anand's book came out about 15 years ago and that those men weren't fascinated.

D: Me too! [Laughter]

B: That's a great book, The Art of Sexual Ecstasy. I remember it well, we were all passing it around, my male and female friends, and you're saying that that didn't happen in your experience.

D: Well, it didn't happen with the partners I had. And I am truthfully still looking for that person who is interested in the experience and integration of spirituality and sexuality. There are many reasons for both men and women to dismiss tantra. Tantra, in my opinion, has a bad rap in our society. It's become associated with orgies and promiscuity, where values are not followed or paid attention to. And that definitely has not been my experience. It's actually the opposite of what's important to me and in what I teach.

B: It's all about intimacy, that's what tantra means to me.

D: Tantra is an ancient practice that has been given to the Western culture through the yogic practices in the Far

East, from India and China. Actually, tantra was developed as a rebellion against that split between the body and the soul. The spiritual traditions of the East also denied the body. Tantra yoga developed as a way for householders to have a spiritual practice in every day life, just as the monks in the monasteries did. It was developed by the householders as a way to honor the body as well as the soul.

B: Interesting. Did you, then, read Margot's book, The Art of Sexual Ecstasy?

D: Yes. I read it, and not only read it, but started going to the workshops by her students, Steve and Lokita Carter, who are really wonderful. They are married and committed to each other, and deeply committed to bringing tantra practices and principles to as many people as possible. I loved the information I got. It was such a perfect fit from the very beginning, and it has taught me so much. I really feel it's been central to my spiritual development. I believe that it has been the source of deep transformation for me.

B: So Steve and Lokita were, from the beginning, excellent teachers in your understanding and growth.

D: Yes, and I specifically chose them because they were a married couple who were very devoted to each other. Even though I was single, I wanted an experience where a couple was modeling how they used tantra in their committed, long term, monogamous relationship.

Prior to going to Steve and Lokita's workshops, I had waited and waited for the right person to come along who wanted to learn about tantra with me, but that person wasn't coming into my life. So I just decided to go as a single. It was a pretty scary decision for me, because even though Steve and Lokita allowed singles to participate in their program, I was afraid it would be mostly married and committed couples, and that I would feel very left out and alone in this work. But I was just not willing to wait any longer. So I entered into the training from a place of my values. And I didn't know if I would have anything to learn as a single person. I thought to myself that at least I will have this for my clients, at the very least I would be able to offer them some of this knowledge. I also hoped to develop skill in tantra, so that I could use it to deepen my relationship with the life partner that I wanted to attract into my life.

B: So, you really took a chance. First of all, you didn't have a partner, and second of all, you weren't that familiar with tantra at that point, when you began going to these workshops.

D: That's right. It was a huge chance, but it was also a huge adventure for me. It was an adventure of the spirit, and also an adventure on an emotional level, because I'm not tremendously comfortable going into groups where it's mostly couples and being on my own. I can feel left out, like I don't belong. But my interest in tantra was big enough and deep enough, that I wanted to do this anyway.

B: Your commitment was great.

D: Yes. I feel that way, and I'm happy to say it's turned out much, much better than I ever imagined it would.

B: Well, tell me about that first time, when you showed up at that first workshop. I'd really like to hear about that.

D: Oh, Bill, it was actually very magical. At the first workshop, there were 10 singles out of a group of 34 people. We chose a new partner for each exercise so I never knew what partner I would have next. This was very challenging to me because I couldn't depend on my partner to help me through these exercises and I didn't get a chance to build a relationship with one person over time. As a result, I learned to depend on myself for support. I learned to open up and act loving because it was my value not necessarily because I was attracted to a man and knew he was attracted to me. This was a huge lesson for me. I realized I had depended on having a primary partner in order to express the vulnerable side of me that I associate with my sexuality. I learned to be vulnerable with different people, sharing personal feelings and information and depending on myself for the emotional and psychological support I had formerly looked for in my male partners.

We did a communication exercise in which we were asked, "Tell me how you like to be loved." I did this exercise with a man, who I had never met before. In the context of doing this work, we first create sacred space and a feeling of safety, where this person in front of me is someone whom I choose to give respect to, and who I also see as someone who cares for me and my well-being, just as much as I am cultivating that caring for him. In this exercise, then, we are seeing that person as our beloved partner. We are encouraged to see that person as the embodiment of the beloved partner that I want to attract and also of the beloved partners I have attracted in my life, who may not be in my life right now. This is a wonderful exercise for couples who have been in relationship for a long time. They come together in the present, and see their partner as someone they want to open their heart to, who they're willing to give their love to, who they're willing to see in the present moment as their deeply beloved partner. This kind of practice encourages people to come right back to the present moment and see the gorgeous, wonder-filled treasure of this person in front of them.

I was asked to share, in any way I wanted, how I liked to be loved. I could share on an emotional level, which is safer: "Well, I like to be loved consistently, responsibly, and respectfully...." Or, if I wanted to, I could say how I wanted to be loved from a physical level, and tell this man where I liked to be touched, how I liked to be touched, and what kind of lovemaking was particularly meaningful and pleasureful for me. I chose to take a risk—and taking risks is exactly what the work in tantra has always inspired me to do. I took the risk to open up, and the opening up was not just to this person in front of me, it was especially to myself. I've learned that every time I open up to someone else, I open my heart to myself, filling my heart, and becoming more intimate with myself, creating my relationship with myself as my own beloved partner, who I walk hand in hand with through life. That's actually been one of the greatest learnings that I've received in my study and practice of tantra: as I open to others, I open to myself; as I open to myself, I open to life.

My whole development through the tantra work I've done—personally, psychologically, and spiritually—has been magnificent beyond words. When I first began going to tantra workshops, I didn't think I could learn a lot more in the area of sexuality, because I've studied this work for 20 years. And yet, that was not the case at all. People at all the workshops I've attended are so open and personal. They bravely and honestly face each other with their issues around their body, about sexuality, about spirituality, about relationship, about intimacy, about self love. I realized from this that I had so much still to learn, and that my study of tantra provided me with all the knowledge and support that I needed to grow psychologically and spiritually, to be my own beloved, my own committed, beloved partner for myself.

B: It sounds to me like the risk-to-benefit ratio is very high. You took a lot of risks, and you received a lot of benefit.

D: Well, yes. And thank you for that observation. I agree that taking risks brings us growth. There is a diagram that I use a lot for my clients about the choices we make in life, about whether to open up or stay closed (See diagram on page 205.) The only way to grow is to choose to open up, and that can be on whatever level I want it to be—emotionally, physically, spiritually, mentally. If we aren't willing to take risks, we tend to defend or protect ourselves in some way. There are three basic ways of doing this: one is to act aggressively, a second way is to withdraw, and a third way is to adapt or pretend that we're okay. An example of adapting or pretending is when somebody asks you how you are, and you feel terrible, and you smile and say, "I'm fine, just fine."

B: That's very common, yes, a very common practice here in America.

D: Right, and so when we defend—and sometimes we may need to do that, or think that we need to—it maintains the status quo, but it doesn't allow us to grow. When we defend or self-protect, we are attempting to create safety in our life. But it is a false safety, and can even ultimately be harmful to us. This is my ongoing challenge in the tantra work: releasing the defenses and self-protecting patterns, and being willing to be seen, to feel some past hurt, to express some deeply held feeling.

Some tantra workshops involve practices in which there is nudity or touching and being touched in a very personal way, but that's always a choice that each participant can make. They are given permission to engage in the practice in the way that feels comfortable to them. So at the beginning of every exercise, there is the question of, "What is my intent? What are my fears? Where are my boundaries?" So, for example, my intention in one of the exercises might be to learn about my energy and how I move energy. My fear would be that I wouldn't feel anything through this exercise.

And then a boundary, which helps me feel safe in regard to any of the fears that I have, might be that I let myself vibrate all over in order to feel the energy, but I'm not willing to allow there to be any touching to my breast or genital areas. So, in that way, when I set my boundaries to help me feel comfortable, then I create safety, and I also give my partner a clear sense of knowing how to support me, as well as what not to do, so that I can feel safe in the process.

B: It seems as though one of the benefits in this is building basic trust. In other words, feeling empowered that you could do something that was healthy, good, and opening for you in these practices, while also feeling trust of the setting and the process.

D: Well, again, it's so wonderful that you bring this up. You're really tuned in to me, because basic trust is another one of those qualities that I've developed during these two years of training. I trust myself, through the work I've done in tantra, to take care of myself, to love myself, to make good choices for myself. And I also trust the universe, meaning whoever is in my presence and whatever is going on. The way I see it is that all I have is the present moment. And so my choice is to take each moment and open up as if this moment and this person in front of me, regardless of who it is, is my beloved partner. In doing so, I develop trust in myself, I create trust with my partner, and I act in trustworthy ways. Further, this allows for genuine contact. There's an experience of feeling alive in the moment, because I'm contacting myself, my own truth, and opening up to who I am. It's as if a bright light is inside that's shining through me, giving me aliveness and an ability to express who I am. Then I experience all of me, as well as my capacity for wholeness, for loving, and for actual bliss.

As a sex therapist, I've received a lot of training about

sexuality and sexual dysfunction, but I was never encouraged to integrate my spiritual life with my sexual life and my sexual functioning, until tantra. With tantra, I've learned to love myself in a deeper way than I ever have before. Tantra is all about seeing the beloved in myself, in others, and in life itself. From that place I can see the beloved, I can see goodness in everything and everyone. Living a tantra lifestyle has empowered me to embrace all of life, to find the good in everything and to accept what happens as a time for learning, a time for growth, a time for giving. I've learned that I'm a lovable, valuable human being. It's also given me clarity about my Catholic upbringing and the ways I was once repressed. Now, I have begun to open up to my life energy, to express it, intensify it, heighten it, and enjoy it more.

Steve and Lokita Carter would describe it as opening to our life energy for the purpose of ecstasy, bliss, and pleasure. In our society, we have been taught to limit pleasure. Put work first, and everything else second. If we have time after work, then we can have time for fun and time for pleasure. Tantra is about integrating pleasure with life and with loving. It has helped me enjoy and support myself with my aliveness, with my joy, with my interest in pleasure, and sharing pleasure with others, including sexual pleasure. I've really grown to learn about the particular techniques that I can use to enhance my sexual pleasure, both by myself and with a partner.

B: So this has been a personal journey of integrating all these different aspects of your life.

D: Right. Very well put. There are so many paths for maturation and growth. I believe that the primary way of waking up, or developing ourselves to be all that we can be, is through awareness. When we are aware of who we really are, we realize we have choices about how to express our aliveness. We also recognize the ways we block our aliveness, and from this place can make choices to resolve those blocks, so we can be all that we can be.

B: That's beautiful, Diana. What a wonderful way of looking at life.

D: It's a wonderful way to embrace and enjoy life.

B: I'm curious: what goals do you have for the future? What else do you have planned for yourself?

D: My purpose for living—and I've done a lot of soul searching to identify this because of my training as a coach— is to be a vehicle of love and healing for myself and others, for life itself, and for the planet herself. I plan to offer a variety of tantra workshops. I gave my first tantra workshop this last spring, and I want to continue to offer this for both couples who are in a committed relationship and for those who are single. I've gone through tantra programs as a 60 year old single woman the last two years, and it's been transformational in my own life. So I want to offer that to other single people, as well as couples. What I plan, then, is to teach tantra, both through retreats as well as through individual and couple coaching, by phone, and in person. I have been doing, as you know, the many interviews of tantra experts and streaming those over the web, the full audio of the interviews. I plan to do more of those. I really believe so much in the tantra path of spiritual awakening, that I want to spread the word as much as possible. So, through my book, recorded interviews, teaching, counseling, coaching, retreats and of course, my own personal practice, I hope to continue being a source of information and inspiration about the life-changing principles of tantra.

B: Yes. That's what's so wonderful about this book, is that it's interspersed with interviews of your teachers.

D: Well, my belief is that if I can grow through tantra,

giving all the experiences I've had in my life, given all the inhibitions, and prohibitions, and negative experiences I've had that have been blocks to integrating spirituality and sexuality, then anyone can. [Laughter] I intend for this book to share my story of my transformation. And then my interviews with Margot, Steve and Lokita, Gaia Reblitz, and Suzie Heumann all give the message that we are not alone. We do not have to live our lives alone, and particularly, we don't have to be alone in this most sacred of areas, the area of sexuality and spirituality, which are considered most personal and private for us. These teachers are truly wonderful; they are principle-centered, value oriented, they come from their hearts, and are truly loving and respectful. This is why they are such fantastic teachers; they can help us grow in these areas by modeling these qualities. Working in these areas of sexuality and spirituality has been the most growthful experience of my entire life, and I want to offer this to others as well.

Chapter 2:

Capacities of Trust & Love

Diana describes ways of transcending our inhibitions
and shame about sexuality and teaches skills to
develop trust in ourselves, our partner and Life
itself, Diana helps us recognize our profound
capacity to love and to open up to passionate
and ecstatic loving through our sexual
experience and expression.

*"Sexuality is an energy that tends toward union; it is the
grounding of our ability to love."*
David Spangler

Bill: I'm seeing, Diana, that there's a theme that flows
through all the interviews you've done with Margot Anand
and the other SkyDancers—and that is an understanding of
basic trust: that we have to have a basic trust around

something before we can fully open to it. One of the things I like about the tantric community in general is that they are making friends with a person's divine right to have incredible, deep experiences of ecstasy and joy. This really is a person's divine right. Making friends with that, knowing that to be true, and approaching it in a non-threatening way perhaps is harder for people to do than I thought. When we're talking about it, it seems so easy.

Diana: Right, Bill. You and I have both studied a very prominent spiritual teacher, A. H. Almaas, also known as Hameed Ali, who has developed the Diamond Approach. Hameed works to help us access spiritual qualities and to experience the essence of who we are, which is the meaning of our soul's journey, our soul's journey home. Hameed says that most of the spiritual work that we do to reach our sense of essence, or wholeness, or the experience of love, really happens in the lower centers—the first and second chakras, which contain the energies of survival and sexuality. When we work on these lower centers, we work directly with our instinctual energies, which are found in our bodies. For there to be a permanent transformation in people's lives—where they really start experiencing what love is, how to live a loving life, and how to be a person of love, a being of love— we have to work on our lower centers of sexuality. Another way of saying this is that we have to open our body. When you do this, Hameed tells us, you will be unencumbered, you will inhabit your body and your being more fully. Your openness will allow your inner essence to emerge; it will empower you to express yourself creatively, in your magnificence.

According to Hameed, the genitals are the center of the physical body, and the freeing of our sexuality is essential to our spiritual realization. When one is sexually liberated, their realization is a palpable, felt experience; it is embodied in the belly, genitals, and pelvis—in the body as a whole. So, although Hameed hasn't taught tantra, he teaches from a perspective of the importance of sexuality to our wholeness, our ability to be loving, and our spiritual transformation. I think that speaks a great deal to the value of tantric principles for our culture and for ourselves.

B: I have studied Hameed's work, and I really admire his fundamental view that we must clear away that which binds and occludes our natural, unbounded self.

D: Yes. The teachings of Hameed are beyond the conceptual realm of the thinking mind. We can study ideas about spiritual unfoldment for a long time without changing or growing one bit. If we only learn mentally, we remain one step removed from it. We tend to analyze it without actually experiencing it. Our minds are great ways of keeping distance from our experience and from our reality. And our minds can tell ourselves a lot of stories that are not true.

On the other hand, tantra programs allow us, through our experience, to grow and change and experience transformation. I've been a sex therapist for thirty years, and during that time I studied sexuality but did not do any of the experiential practices found in tantra. When I began to actually experience some of these exercises, such as letting go of body armoring or taking off my clothes in a workshop, there was a whole new dimension of learning and understanding available to me. There are many, many messages of shame and negativity and a control that have been given to us over the years that we store in our genitals. These can be felt and healed by the experience of our bodies, not so much when we merely think about the traumatic material.

Here's a wonderful example, something that happened in a

tantra workshop. At this workshop, we had worked together for many days, and for one exercise, we were invited—not told—to sit in a small group of two women and two men and to take off whatever clothes we felt comfortable with. We were then invited to stand up in the middle of this group and talk about what we liked about our bodies and what we didn't, what we were ashamed of and what were upset about. Then we received feedback from the other three people in our group, who we had grown to know and trust deeply through much personal sharing. I remember talking about my dislike of my wrinkles, around my face. When they gave feedback, the men said that the wrinkles in my face were like sunshine lines and laugh lines that really expressed the light of my soul. I have never seen the wrinkles in my face the same way since.

That experience of two men who were new friends, but very loving, respectful people, tell me that they loved my wrinkles because it expressed the essence of what my life has been, that they saw the light in my face through my wrinkles—and that they saw light, energy and joy in my body from the inside out—is a gift that I'll have forever. So to have experienced that kind of human sharing and support about my body was priceless.

Here's another example, from my own practice. I have recently been working with a man in the sex therapy I do. He has been married 40 years, and he's coming in now, at over 70 years of age with an interest in healing and revitalizing his somewhat lifeless sexual relationship with his wife. I found it interesting when he said that his wife is a former nun, a Catholic nun. She left the convent and ended up marrying him years and years ago. But the area of their sex life has been very repressed and, because of that, their own aliveness has become repressed, distorted, and limited.

When people aren't able to express themselves in open, truthful and personal ways, their sex life gets dull, boring, and bland. This man said in our therapy work, "Our sex life is flat. My wife told me two years ago that she didn't want me to touch her sexually anymore." So for two years, he was saying, he hasn't touched his wife sexually. And now, he says, "I don't want to live this way. I don't want my life to be dead." But this is a man who really believes in, and feels good about, sexuality as a part of his life. And, certainly, he wants it to be a part of his marriage.

The tantra work I'm going to do with him and his wife will hopefully be a vehicle that will allow them to go beyond where they've been for 40 years. When people start seeing the body as love, as life, as goodness, as a vehicle for expressing love, expressing who we really are, then their whole sexual relationship opens up and becomes free. In this openness and freedom, they both agree that anything that is good for the two of them is something that they want to express and experience. They will want to integrate deeper experience and greater closeness into their sexual relating.

B: It's interesting to me that they've been together this long, 40 years, in a committed relationship.

D: And she's been very inhibited. She has only wanted certain ways of relating sexually, and only tolerated and accepted that, and a lot was just completely off limits. I don't know for sure, because I'm just starting to work with them, but things such as oral genital sex was probably off limits, as well as anal sex, and I bet certain positions. So for her, there were just certain ways of expressing sexually that were comfortable. When these kinds of limits are set, then a person starts limiting their own experience of who they are, and limiting their own expression of who they are, as well as their partner's.

B: And isn't it also true, Diana, that repression is acted out in other parts of a person's life?

D: That can happen, definitely. I can think of two other situations that I'm dealing with right now in my sex therapy work where there are difficulties in the relationship that have not been talked about. Part of those difficulties have to do with differences in sex desire, and that's very typical. That's actually the biggest problem that couples have in relating sexually. So, instead of talking about that and working that out in a couple's relationship, they've pretty much kept it inside. They haven't talked about it, but have gotten more and more unhappy, more and more out of touch with what feels good to them, and more distant as a couple. In one of the cases I'm working with, a couple was with some friends, another couple, and they were all drinking a lot. At one point, the husband went into another room with his friend's wife, and they started making out. All of a sudden, they were having sex. Then this man's wife got suspicious, and went in and found them. They came in for therapy not long after that incident.

So what's gone wrong? What's happened? We discovered that they needed to talk about their differences in sex desire and their differences in sexual preferences, as well as some of the other problems they were having that they really hadn't brought out in the open. All of this happened because of unhappiness and unmet needs that weren't talked about, expressed, or resolved. I could go on with story after story where this is the case.

B: So that's a real example of acting out from a place of not finding sexual intimacy.

D: Exactly. And it's not just the sexual intimacy that was at issue, because sexuality, as you know, is a representation of intimacy on every level; it's multifaceted. So women, particularly, will say that their sexual intimacy starts far earlier than foreplay or intercourse. For them, sexual intimacy begins with a, "Good morning, hello," as they first get out of bed in the morning, a goodbye kiss, and maybe a warm hug when they both meet again in the evening. In this way, sexuality is a lifelong, daily, moment-to-moment experience, where one learns how to make love in their every day moments, as well as in the bedroom when they are relating sexually.

B: Well, I remember Steve and Lokita Carter once saying that a yawn is an orgasm, stretching the body is an orgasm. [Laughter] It seems to me that you're talking about all those things.

D: Well, the definition that Steve and Lokita give for orgasm is that it's an involuntary redistribution of energy. So, actually, it is the flowing of energy through the body, and our sexual energy is probably the biggest energy we have, besides anger. Anger and sexuality are two really strong energies that we experience.

B: And haven't you said, Diana, that anger and sexuality are located close to each other in the brain?

D: Yes, the centers of sexuality and anger are quite close. That explains why, after a fight or an argument, a couple often feel sexually aroused. Their anger stimulates their interest in sex. And touching and sexual intercourse and orgasm stimulate the brain to produce serotonin and norepinephrine that elevate the mood and produce a natural high. Orgasm also produces the chemical oxytocin that bonds people to each other. So sex and orgasm deepen intimacy.

The counterpoint to this is that it happens when people are not in love. So I would suggest that if you don't want to fall in love with a person, don't have sex with them.

B: Fascinating.

D: Yes, it is.

B: And it seems to me that again, what we're really talking about here is the notion of basic trust, which is a deep, abiding trust in the goodness, the essential okay-ness, of your own body, your sexuality, your energies, and your emotions. That, in fact, our body experiences are organic and natural, and are not something to fear or repress. Our feelings and sexuality actually allow us, it seems, to contact ourselves and others and to explore new frontiers of experience, pleasure, and joy.

D: Yes, I think that's a wonderful way of summarizing it, Bill. I love your astute and wise way of looking at this. I would add that we're talking about basic trust in sexuality as our capacity for loving. David Spangler, who's a spiritual channel, teacher, and educator, talks about sexuality as the grounding of our ability to love. I think that sexuality and spirituality are very interrelated, and that we need to trust our capacity to love our sexuality as a God-given, natural gift that we have. It is a blessing and a gift to develop and cultivate. It's also an energy that tends towards unity, so it actually offers us the ability to not be alone, to be connected with all of life, and to really go towards what we're attracted to for our happiness and ecstasy and bliss, as the tantra work would call it.

B: Isn't part of your work as a tantrika, Diana, the incredible joy and bliss that comes from dissolving boundaries?

D: From dissolving boundaries and loving without fear, loving without limits. And there's great joy in accepting the body as a center of sacredness and wisdom just as the soul is. The body is really a mirror of the soul, a vessel of the soul, a vehicle for expressing the soul. We can live in both worlds. We live on the earth, and we are spiritual beings expressing as humans. We are of heaven and of the earth both. To honor our sexuality is to honor our ability to love and our ability to be in our bodies at the same time. And that's always a balancing act, and it's why the subject, in my opinion, is so controversial, and yet so necessary to talk about.

B: If you look at it strictly from a scientific standpoint, the genitals are an organ just like the ears, the eyes, or the mouth. Because I'm an astrophysicist I've often thought, "Well, wouldn't it be interesting if a person's genitals were on the right side of their cheek? Or if they were on their neck?" Then there would probably be all kinds of issues about that part of the body. And if people's mouths between their legs, then that area of the body may not be so hidden.

D: Right. I think that there's a tremendous amount of social, religious, and even political overlay to our expression of our sexuality and our experience of our genitals. As a result, there are so many restrictions, limitations, inhibitions, and shame associated with our genitals and sexuality, that we have inhibited our expression of sexuality and of loving. Having limited these essential aspects of our life, so many people are crying for more meaning, more connection, and more experience of soul in our lovemaking. For that reason, I think tantra work is very important. The only person we really have full responsibility for, the only person we're able to control, is ourselves. We are the ones who can bring back these lost pieces; we do this in our own life by becoming more open, more loving, more willing to connect and have soulful experiences. And, very importantly, more loving toward ourselves. We love ourselves first, and only from that place can we deeply love another—whether it's our primary partner, our children, our parents, or our friends.

B: Also perhaps when we demystify the sexual experience, both positively and negatively. In all parts of our society, sexuality has become commercialized and mystified and reduced to physical appearances. I remember when I was a young recording engineer working with super models. They were pretty perfect—that was their job, to be perfect.

And they would have cosmetic surgery to make sure they were perfect. Yet, underneath they hated themselves. In other words, they had not done this basic piece of work to help them love themselves more.

D: Hameed has spoken so beautifully to this: that, if we look outside of ourselves for gratification or fulfillment, we'll always be lacking. So, in that regard, it's not, "How can we measure up to some standard of beauty in society?" It's, "How can I live in my body? How can I love my genitals and be sexually expressive in the way that is right for me? How can I do that with integrity? How can I fully enjoy my body, express as my body, express as my genitals, express as my soul?" When I express my body and my soul, I live in both worlds. I live as a human being, and I live as a spiritual being, in that balance and in that tension. That's what being human and being spiritual is all about, in my opinion.

B: It is, then, an inner journey of your own experience, your own sensations. It's not so much outer-directed as it is experiencing deeper and deeper parts of yourself; continually deepening and expanding sexual experience with yourself.

D: Well, yes, it is about our inner experience, not what we may be out in the world. In my case, there are two qualities of my worldly self that are considered by our society as not fully fulfilled or successful. I'm single, and have been single for ten years, and I'm 60 years old. It used to be, and it still may be, that single women who are my age were considered either unmarryable, dried out, over the hill, unattractive, and all of that.

At the same time, my experience of being 60 is wonderful. Being single has helped me reference myself as my primary partner, my primary Beloved. And that, actually, is what all of us are called to do, but it's not easy to do if one is in a primary relationship. When I was married, I remember depending on my partner to love me. As long as he loved me, I felt lovable, and I didn't have to reference myself as a source of trust or love. It's only as a single person, when I was forced to do that, that I've done it.

Tantra called me to open up on a physical level as well as a spiritual level. I didn't have to do that, but in doing it I have grown tremendously—psychologically and spiritually. I feel better about myself and about my body, and I feel more able to express myself and my soul. The openness works. I can name so many experiences of this through my work. Tantra has deepened my experience of loving and trusting both myself and the goodness of life.

Chapter 3:

Ecstatic Loving & Living

A conversation with Steve and Lokita Carter about
the relationship between love, sexuality, spirituality
and intimacy. They describe the differences between
men & women and how to bridge those differences.

Diana: Steve and Lokita Carter, my friends and my teachers,
have a wonderful program called Ecstatic Living as well as many
other programs on sexuality that are wonder-filled and truly
growthful. I've participated in three of their programs, and I'm
delighted to have the opportunity to speak with them about
their work, their purpose and mission, and their vision for doing
this work. So, thank you very much for being here, you two.

Steve: Thank you for inviting us.

D: You describe your Ecstatic Living program as: "Weaving
the integration of love, sex, and spirituality into the fabric of our
life." Would you tell me what that means?

S: 'Ecstatic living'—that's a very broad term, isn't it? And that's what we think tantra is. It includes all aspects of our lives. Now a lot of times in our lives, we don't expand our joy, expand our being; we limit what we feel, what we create, and what we do. In Ecstatic Living, we don't want to limit anything. We want to expand ourselves and live at our full potential, with as much joy and bliss as possible in our lives.

Lokita: Ecstatic Living does integrate love, sex, and spirituality into the fabric of our daily life. So often, we forget that spirituality is a part of our daily life. We will have sex, but often times we have sex just to release some energy or to re-create ourselves. With the approach of Ecstatic Living, we integrate sex with spirituality and, of course, with love. We bring all of these facets of our experience into our day to day life. And all that woven together makes for a very rich life experience.

D: I'm impressed with your emphasis on the integration of love, sex, and spirituality. Many of the critics of tantra talk about tantra as simply 'getting off' sexually—making it an excuse for intensifying our experience of orgasm or ejaculation or sexual energy. What's your response to that critique of tantra?

S: Well, the media has kind of blown tantra out of proportion. If you look at most popular magazines, you might see a magazine article titled: "Tantra: The Seven Steps to the Biggest Orgasm." This doesn't portray tantra in the full sense of what it really is. Tantra is a spiritual path that includes sexuality. But the majority of the work in tantra doesn't have anything to do with sex. Sex can be used as a doorway to get an "Ah hah," to get a realization about what spirituality is, what connection with another person is, what beautiful communication is, and about not being separate in your own life. So when we practice tantra, we use sexuality as sort of a hand-hold to be able to reach up, open this doorway a little bit, get a breath of fresh air, and say, "God, maybe I could create some of that openness and love in my normal life." If I was going to communicate with a friend, I could look into their eyes directly; I could have a direct communication.

D: That sounds wonderful. I was going to ask you the question: How do you use this experience of sexuality to heighten spirituality? You started answering by talking about how you breathe and look into a person's eyes. Would you please say more about some of the practices that will heighten that integration of sexuality, spirituality, and love?

S: In tantric sexuality, the picture we use is like a staircase: we come up to a level of near orgasm, and then we use our tools—movement, breath, sound, and presence—to begin to expand our energy. The envelope that we hold ecstatic energy in gets bigger; it gets to be a whole-body experience, rather than just centered on the genitals. So if we breathe, we're able to expand that energy. If we make sound, if we are present, we're able to be more and more expansive in our experience.

D: Oh, that's beautiful.

L: The integration of love, spirituality, and sexuality goes even a little bit further than how we can expand through breath, movement, and presence. If I think about the integration of those, spirituality is generally a concept that's pretty lofty and removed from the body. You know, you go the church and pray, but what does that really have to do with the body? Sure, it's a form of spiritual worship or spiritual service, but it doesn't really include our physical reality. In tantra and Ecstatic Living, the reality is that we do have a body, and the body has a variety of different functions in our lives. And one of the functions, for me, is that it holds the spirit that we are. The body is the temple of our spirit, and so tantra is a spiritual path that sees the body as a vehicle of spirituality.

Now spirituality includes everything. It doesn't just include worshiping in the church or doing special things—bringing the divine into the body—but it also includes things that we do with our body to express ourselves. If we sing a beautiful song, or plant a beautiful garden of flowers, or paint a sunset, whatever these things are that we're creating with our body are beautiful pieces of art. In tantra, lovemaking is seen as an art, as an art form that we do with our body as a form of spiritual service, if you want to call it that.

D: You sure are provoking a lot of thinking on my part, as you've done in the workshops I've attended with you in the past. I'm curious, are you saying that there is nothing bad or wrong in the whole area of tantra as a spiritual path? Often, the church and society will define a right way and a wrong way for us to express ourselves sexually, or how we can relate sexually. So I'm curious about the whole concept of right and wrong, good and bad when it comes to tantra.

S: In tantra, we believe in acceptance. Acceptance of who you are, who I am, and who everyone else is. That process of acceptance allows everyone to become a little bit closer. That doesn't mean that, with acceptance, you have to like somebody, or that you have to agree with somebody. But you can just see who that person is. Now along with acceptance, we must consider the word 'judgment,' which I think you were talking about. There might be a lot of judgment by society or religion about some particular actions. In tantra, we want to live consciously, but we want to accept how people are. Part of that word 'acceptance' is that it's not very easy to accept, sometimes, who we are or who other people are. But if we do that, we allow the universe and the magic of life to bring us from one moment to the next moment. Because when we do....

Excuse me, my wife is just shaking her head, "No, no, no." So you can cut that part out, and I'm going to continue on because it's very distracting when she does that.

D: [Laughter]

S: Anyway, I'm going to start over again.

D: Actually, I would like to leave that part in, because you two—I wanted to say this at the beginning of our discussion—are really wonderful role models of a married couple who are very committed to each other, and committed to your relationship. You use your relationship as a way of growing into loving more deeply and more fully. What you just typified to me, right now, is that honesty is a big part of what you both are committed to, and you'll be totally honest with each other. That's given me the permission to be honest with myself and with my primary partner, as well as with other people in my life. I thank you for that example.

S: You know what? What you're talking about is a tantric lifestyle. You're living honestly, and you're saying the truth. That's what we do in tantra. When we say acceptance of yourself and others, you also have to give yourself permission to say, "Yes, that is my truth."

D: Mmm.

S: When somebody asks you to the movies or something, do you want to be nice and say, "Well, I feel obligated. I'll go"? But if you didn't want to go, that would be a "No."

D: Right.

S: But you said "Yes." So you want to say "Yes" for your truth always. Of course, you look at the circumstances: you're not going to be totally centered on just your own feelings, but you're going to take into account everything around you. Being able to accept and say "Yes" for your truth, for what really is, is a huge gift and a huge healing not only for yourself, but also for those around you.

D: You talk about being in your truth, and I appreciate that so much. At the same time, there are so many problems or conflicts that come up with couples around sexuality. Things like different desire levels in people, and the issue of frequency. Some women who I work with don't have orgasms, and they feel really guilty about that. And some men either have premature ejaculation or delayed ejaculation. So there are all of these experiences of guilt, of what's right and what's wrong, that create a lot of pain with the whole area of sexuality. How does tantra relate to and deal with these issues?

S: When we practice tantra, one of the first things we teach people is how to make your sacred space. We believe that a sacred space is where two people can come together, not be disturbed by the outside, and give their full attention to being together. Normally, in our lives, the phone is ringing, the dogs are barking, the mail man is coming, your work is on your mind, so a lot of the time, people can't really focus on what they need and want. To be able to create a sacred space and to be present with yourself and your partner, gives a huge healing and allows people to connect together. First we teach people the basic tools of intimacy, then—when they accomplish that—they can make love.

L: You mentioned all of these different concerns and issues, Diana, that arise in sexuality. In tantra, the way we understand it, there is no goal in sex. In tantra, basically, the journey is the goal. We don't have to go off 'over there' to this big, fantastic orgasm with the perfect timing, or the perfect length, or the perfect intensity, or all the rest of that. Instead, we say that you've got to enjoy the journey, because we don't know where the journey is going to lead. If we focus all our energy, all our intention on some goal—like having that particular orgasm—then we get so goal-oriented that we can't see certain things. The small moments are not so meaningful anymore, because suddenly, all we can think of is that big 'O' somewhere in the distance. That's how, I think, we address these particular issues. Our work is to encourage people to become more aware of the journey, and to be more in the here and now. As Steve said, we create a sacred space, and we have communication in the present, in the here and now. "How does something feel right now?" Rather than, "I wish in five minutes I could come."

D: I took in a big sigh as you were talking, I feel myself relaxing, I have this smile on my face, and I'm just appreciating. The context that you're creating is so honoring of the sexual experience and union. I just love what we're talking about, and it's a real privilege to experience that with you two. The question that's coming up for me now is, "What does love have to do with all this?"

S: Love has to do with everything, because that's who you are, girl! [Laughter] Much of the time, we get side-tracked with the idea that we're something else besides love. Your essence is love, as mine is. The pure light force energy is love. So love has to do with everything, because if we start leading our lives through our hearts, and connecting about what our truth is, you're going to live and love. You're going to live in a conscious lifestyle that promotes openness and expansion. So love has everything to do with tantra and everything to do with life.

D: I knew I could count on you, Steve, to give me the answer. [Laughter]

S: [Laughter] Now, let me tell you something else.

D: Okay, go for it.

S: Creating a sacred space: that is like ritual. In our

society, nowadays, ritual has basically been forgotten. Of course, we celebrate birthdays, anniversaries, and graduation. But there are a lot of things that we need rituals for that are just small and simple. When we create a sacred space, we're performing a ritual. Another ritual is coming together with your lover for an occasion, and that occasion doesn't have to be a big occasion—it could be simply, "Let's sit down and have a talk together." You could create a little ritual to connect up, using proper communication tools. We also like to teach about energy—how to make energy move in the body. A lot of people aren't even familiar with energy. They'll say, "Well what do you mean? Is it PG&E (Pacific Gas and Electric) or what?" [Laughter] But there is energy in our bodies, energy around our bodies, and energy that we share with each other all the time in our lives. Like when we're making love: when we get a lot of energy around our genitals, we're very aware of that! [Laughter]

D: Yes, we are! I am! [Laughter]

S: We want to be able to expand that energy. How you move energy is just with your intention. Now, in tantra, there's a whole energy system, which has to do with the Inner Flute and the chakras, the energy centers in the body. We teach you how to move energy throughout the energy system, so you begin to be able to expand your energy. Once you learn more about energy, you can expand your own energy, and you can share that energy with a partner. When you do that, it's more like a soul-to-soul, spirit-to-spirit connection that you can have with your partner, your lover, or your friend.

D: I feel so good about a couple of experiences that I've had in your workshops. One was bringing up, through the breath and through movement, the energy from my pelvis, my first and second chakras, to my 6th and 7th chakras, the areas in the middle of my forehead and above my head. There was this feeling I had of strong energy that was very pleasurable in my pelvis. As I moved that energy up to my heart, and then moved it up to my head and beyond to my connection with the universe, there was this feeling of actual ecstasy—what I think you're talking about. I felt so open, free, and connected with my partner; and he was having a similar experience. We had eye contact during this whole encounter. We hardly had any physical contact, but there was contact with the energy of feeling all of this love rising into my heart, and then there was this feeling of oneness. Is that what you're talking about?

S: Exactly. The amazing thing is, a lot of times people think that they have to have sex to have a feeling like that.

D: Mmm.

S: But you don't. You had an experience where you had almost no physical contact. You could have had no physical contact at all, and you would have had that exact, ecstatic feeling in your whole body, without having sex. Tell us, Lokita, what is the definition of an orgasm?

L: The definition of an orgasm is the involuntary redistribution of energy.

S: I'll just stretch and yawn, and that's an orgasm. In our life, in our society, we've taken that word, 'orgasm,' and associated it with only the genitals or sex. In tantra, we want to bring that word 'orgasm' into our life, so we can be orgasmic beings. We can be more orgasmic. Not necessarily more genital orgasms, but more whole-body orgasms—where you can see a flower, or smell a flower, and get an ecstatic feeling through your whole body. You might even call that a 'full body orgasm.' Or you could drink a cup of tea and have an orgasm. Now you have the choice. If you become aware of how to move your energy through your body, it doesn't mean that every time you smell a flower or drink a cup of tea, you're going to have an orgasm. You can choose to be orgasmic or not, depending on your surroundings.

D: I'm really getting a flavor of ecstasy and pleasure through what you're talking about, and I'm feeling it in my body as we talk. I have a question...

S: Well, you're such an evolved being! [Laughter]

D: Oh, gosh. I'm ready to take more of your workshops!

I'm curious about the difference between men and women. As a woman, I know I've focused so much on love in order to feel sexually aroused, sexually open, and sexually connected to my partner. If that feeling of love isn't there, I'm just not too interested in sharing sexuality with a person.

I know from the work I do, that a lot of men feel that they don't have their heart open until they feel that sexual energy. When they can connect sexually, then their heart opens and they feel closer, more connected, and more spiritually unified with their partner. Do you find these differences with men and women? What's your experience in dealing with the gender differences?

S: In our society—in the work place, a lot of times— people don't really notice the energetic difference between men and women. Women will be doing the same jobs as men, having the same responsibilities, and the difference of man and woman is not noted in some aspects of our lives. In our workshops, a lot of times we'll separate the men and the women for an exercise. When a group of men get together and when the women get together, the difference in the energy when we come back together feels like, "Well, that's what that distinct male and female energy is all about." Of course, in the energetic body of a male, the energetic positive pole is the penis. In the energetic body of a female, the positive pole is the heart. So the integration of sex and spirit, of sex and heart, brings those two polarities together. So there are definitely differences between men and women. In tantra, we become more aware of what the differences are and of how to come together in our differences with awareness.

D: Lokita, do you have anything to add to that?

L: Well, I would say exactly the same thing that Steve just said. And I would probably add to that that, in our workshops, we also suggest that people should honor the differences—honor the difference that the man opens his heart through just having sex, while the woman has to have the open heart to have a more fulfilling sexual experience.

So we have ways to honor that: the man can perform special rituals or do special things to open the heart of the woman first, even though he was already set and ready for a bit more sexual contact for this time together—and the other way around. We can have time that we set aside to give our partner what they need—instead of just saying, "Ah, well, we're just different, and that's the way it is." We also have a process where we consciously bring together the different energetic poles. Like Steve said, the male positive pole is his genitals, and for the female, it's the heart. The female negative energetic pole is her genitals, and the male negative energetic pole is his heart. In a particular meditation that we call 'The Breath of Love,' we bring those negative and positive poles together—not necessarily inside of each other, in terms of the genitals, unless people want to do that in the privacy of their room. But we learn to bring energy from the heart, the positive pole of the woman, into the negative pole of the man, his heart, so that he can share with her his positive pole. We create an energetic circle so that these dualities disappear. (See diagram on page 203.)

S: I would like to add something to that. If we create a

sacred space, and create a ritual when we come together, one of the things we can do in that sacred space is ask or state to each other what our desires, our fears, and our boundaries are. If we were to sit down together, and we were thinking about making love, or getting a massage, or communicating—it doesn't make any difference what it is—I would state my desire, I would state my fear, and then I would state my boundary. That way, my partner knows exactly where I'm coming from. Let's say I said, "I want to make love, my fear is you won't want to make love, and my boundary is we do it tonight." [Laughter]

D: [Laughter]

S: And let's say she says, "Well, my desire is to be intimate, my fear is all you want to do is make love, and my boundary is..."—what would be Lokita's boundary? I can't think of one. Lokita might say her boundary is....

L: "You can't come inside of my body."

S: Okay. [Laughter]

L: "You can make love with me in different ways, but not there."

S: If she said that, because we are spiritual beings, I would honor her. I would find a way where I attended to her desires, fears, and boundaries, and we would round down to the less intimate level, where we could actually connect together. Once we make that connection, who knows what's going to happen? The male sexuality is a little bit warmer—his sexuality is ready to boil more quickly than the female sexuality. The female sexuality takes a little warming, right? A little playfulness, a little communication, a little fun, and all those other things, before her heart and her yoni—her vagina—open. The man's genitals are usually ready all the time. [Laughter]

D: [Laughter] I am so touched by how you just shared a

practice and a belief system that takes away any sense of manipulation, control, or conflict in a relationship. I hear such an honoring of each person's essence and each person's desires, fears, and boundaries. Often in the sex therapy that I do, I've heard women talk about feeling used by a man, that a man wants to just 'get off' and uses his partner for that. This practice sounds like it transforms any of those conflicts, because there's honoring of the essence of each person.

S: That's right exactly.

D: So, I'm curious, would you talk a bit about how tantra has affected your personal relationship? You've been married for how long now?

L: For six years we've been together.

D: Six years.

L: Yes. We got married about two months after we met.

D: My goodness. And you've both been practitioners of tantra for a long time before that, right?

L: Yes. I've been practicing and studying since my late teens, actually, so when I met Steve, I already had quite a few years of experience and practice under my belt—no pun intended on that one. [Laughter] That's quite a few years of experience in tantra already, so, as far as my life is concerned, tantra has always been a big part of it—sexually and spiritually, in my everyday life. That's why we've coined that phrase, the 'tantric lifestyle.'

When Steve and I met some six and a half years ago, we met as two people who had individually practiced and played for a long time with tantra. Our relationship basically began in the tantric context. We had a training with Margot Anand that was the first activity that we ever did together as a couple. That was two weeks into us knowing each other. So, for us and our relationship, we basically started out with these premises and tenets of tantra. We can communicate to each other our desires, fears, and boundaries. We share our needs, we have rituals, and we have these different practices that we integrated into the relationship right from the start. That doesn't mean that our relationship has always been like the sweetest honey, because we're two dynamic people with our own different stories and our own different desires. So I can say that the tools we have in our tantric treasure chest, particularly the communication and ritual, has really helped us to overcome the conflicts that are quite common in a relationship—like control issues or 'who's the boss.' There are a whole wealth of treasures that we can use from tantra to overcome that.

D: How wonderful.

L: For us, those things work very well. That also reminds me to say that tantra isn't something that happens in the bedroom only—I think we touched upon that a bit earlier. Tantra is something that really includes everything we do. It includes our work, it includes our daily life together, how we relate to each other when we cook a meal, how we are when we go for a walk with the dogs, and how present we are. For me, that's where the love comes in. The love is something that's really a big, big concept, and at the same time it's a very small and simple thing. Love can be like the smallest moment. This is all part of it. Living in a tantric relationship and bringing this tantric work out into the world through our Timeless Loving program is really an empowering thing, for me personally, for us and our relationship, and for all these people we're working with, like yourself.

D: Your lives are such a tribute to the essence of tantra and the blessing that tantra has for all of us. Steve, would you be willing to share anything else that tantra has meant to you personally and in your relationship with Lokita?

S: As Lokita was saying: "It's the journey, not the goal." That has transformed my life in a million different ways, because it brought me more into present time. So many times in the past, I was looking to the goal; in lovemaking I was thinking, "I want to have a big orgasm." In my life, I might have been thinking, "I want to sell this house." All of my energy would be out there in a real estate deal or something like that, and not more in the moment. Even though I still will always want a big orgasm [laughter], and I still would like to have that goal out there—selling the house—the moment-by-moment steps in life are such a treat, because I have more time to enjoy each moment. That has probably been the biggest transformation of my life.

The other thing is to be able to really recognize what spirituality is. In the past, I was always thinking, "God…. All these spiritual beings…. What does it really take to be a spiritual being?" Through tantra, I actually experience—in my body—my spirit, the spirits of other people, that connection, and that love. I've realized that in my body, just in my body alone, I am a spiritual being. All I have to do is take the time to recognize what my essence is. So this understanding, too, has changed my life in many, many, many ways.

D: Would one of you tell us about the programs you have coming up and how our readers can reach you if they want to get a hold of you and learn more about your programs?

L: I can do that. As I mentioned before, we have the Timeless Loving seminars. These are seminars designed for couples and singles. We have the Level I, which is a gentle introduction to tantra. There, we bring forth the principles and keys of the tantra, as we see it, by teaching ritual, communication, and doing work together. That's a seminar that's open to couples and singles. We also have a Level II seminar that deals with pelvic body work. In that seminar, we learn to be really focused with our partner as we give them a pelvic body work session, which means a massage in the area of the genitals. Now the focus of that seminar is not arousal, it's more focused on healing—healing any somatic or physical holding that may be there in the body from a variety of different experiences. We have also a Level III, which is a seminar for couples on multiple orgasms for men and women—or should I say, for women, and, yes, for men as well! Men can also have multiple orgasms!

D: Yes!

L: This is the seminar that everyone wants to go to first. But you have to begin by learning all these different keys to work with your energy, communication, and presence before you can really tackle the subject of multiple orgasm. But in that workshop, I'd say 99% of everyone who comes there experiences multiple orgasmic sensations in one way or another. In this workshop, we work with those tantric elements to spread the pleasure and expand the pleasure throughout the whole body, and then we irrigate ourselves with this ecstasy so that we can come to a point of spiritual ecstasy and merging with our partner. There, the line between giving and receiving disappears; you give pleasure and you receive pleasure all at the same time.

S: My favorite workshop is an annual workshop we do. At the end of the year, we go to Costa Rica and we practice tantra in a fabulous retreat center. We eat incredibly beautiful food, we take little trips to explore the waterfall gardens, we go white-water rafting 22 miles down a river, we do a lot of really, really fun things. After that workshop, we take a bus—if anyone wants to attend; not the whole workshop usually does—and go explore a little bit of some other parts of Costa Rica. We visit some hot springs, the ocean, the beaches, this and that. That's my favorite workshop, because we get to spend a lot of time with everybody and have a lot of fun.

D: Well, it seems to me that you two live out the lessons of your ecstatic, loving workshops. You live them out in your lives and in your relationship, and I give you credit and a real tribute for the way you're changing the world by changing yourselves. You're certainly influencing me and those that you touch.

S: Oh, you're so kind.

D: Please give us your web address and phone number.

L: You can visit our website at www.ecstaticliving.com or call us toll free at 877-982-6872.

D: Wonderful, thank you. If anyone has any questions about your work, I encourage them to contact you.

L: Yes, that would be very welcomed. People can call us anytime. We'll be more than happy to answer any questions. We sit here at the other end of the phone with an open heart and a big smile. [Laughter]

D: Oh, and that is the truth! I can testify to that personally, so thank you, again, so much. Bless you both.

L: Thank you.

S: Thank you, Diana.

Chapter 4:

Eight Secrets to a Great Love Life

An interview with Margot Anand about the Art of
Sexual Connection, Awakening the Wild Self, and
other practices that kindle ecstatic sexuality.

Diana: It is my privilege and pleasure to introduce my
teacher, workshop facilitator, and friend, Margot Anand.
Margot has facilitated the workshop I just completed, called
The Art of Sexual Ecstasy for Women Over 45. We had a
wonderful nine days of personal sharing and bathing in the
wisdom and the personal example that Margot shared
through her stories, her teaching, and her life. I have grown
to respect Margot as a wonderful teacher, and a woman who
is teaching me and so many people that growing older is

growing better. I think, Margot, that you show us how to live in such a juicy and wonderful way. I'm so pleased and proud to have you share your wisdom and your wit with us.

Margot: Wonderful, thank you, I'm honored.

D: I know that you have just returned from a terrific time with Tony Robbins in Fiji, where he was working with 27 couples in a workshop called Ultimate Passion. Also, you've been working on your new book, Eight Secrets to a Great Love Life. So, Margot, you are one busy woman and certainly have a lot of wisdom to share with us.

M: Thank you, I'm so pleased to spend time with you.

D: I'd like to begin by talking about some basics to give our readers a frame of reference. You have written several books: The Art of Sexual Ecstasy, The Art of Sexual Magic, The Art of Orgasm, and The Art of Everyday Ecstasy. These books are extraordinary, in-depth guides to sacred sexuality. Your SkyDancing School of Tantra has also been a tremendous resource to the student of tantra. I'm curious, Margot, during these many years of exploring, writing, and teaching, what have you experienced as the fundamental meaning of tantra and what does the SkyDancing School teach about tantra?

M: The general meaning of tantra—and you know there are many meanings to the word tantra—the root Sanskrit word translates as 'expanding' and 'weaving.' In my teaching, I like to give a broad definition that says, "Choose with awareness what brings you joy and that opens the door to your spirit."

This is a general philosophy and perspective of tantra, which says that you grow in choosing consciously what brings you pleasure, because then your spirit feels welcome in your body and your heart sings. This applies to sexuality, it applies to love, it applies to how you lead your daily life, it applies to your conversations, whether you choose to focus on problems or on appreciations about what does work in your life. It applies to many, many different things, because tantra is actually a philosophy and a spiritual path like yoga or Zen. The only difference is that tantra includes sexuality as a door to awakening in its dimensions, whereas most of the other spiritual paths say that we have to give up or transcend sex.

So, here in tantra, and specifically in SkyDancing tantra, we explain that the very height of sexual experience is like a meditation, because it propels you to a place that is beyond your ego or personality, or your do's and don'ts, or your mental interferences. You're just simply, totally present in the now and in a great big flow of energy, carried by your breath. Your pleasure brings you to a paroxysm of intense energy, and when you let go totally, you have a glimpse of the ecstatic dimension and a glimpse of your connection to God and to Goddess.

So in that sense it is said in the ancient Vedic texts, that the Vedic seers and the yogis of old actually had the first notion of spiritual enlightenment when they practiced orgasmic lovemaking and developed the yoga of love. There is a very deep link between lovemaking and meditation, which most people haven't a clue about in this country and in this culture. Most people who pretend to teach tantra don't even practice true tantra. We don't have a lifestyle in America now that really allows us to practice tantra to the fullest.

D: What do you mean, Margot?

M: Well, the tantric yogic path, if it's really practiced, requires easily five hours.

D: Ah.

M: When I get together with my tantric beloved, we start with food and the preparation of the food, and then we go to yoga, and we find the right environment to practice yoga and the yoga asanas that specifically awaken sexual energy. We practice meditation facing each other, seeing each other as divine. Then we bless each other, and we invoke the spirit in each others' bodies. There are many, many steps that teach us erotic devotion and honoring of each other and bring the divine archetype into our minds and hearts so that when we look at our partner, we can see Shiva, we can see Shakti, we can see the Godhead. (Shiva and Shakti are Hindu names for the Godhead.) When we are able to do that, suddenly our whole perspective of who we're looking at and how we address them shifts. We see in them all the infinite potential that they carry within themselves, because God to me means simply the existence of an intelligence that has infinite ability to create.

D: What a wonderful perspective.

M: So, the infinitely creative is manifesting itself through this body and this being at this time. And the more we know how to play with this energy consciously, the more the divine is going to be delighted to manifest itself.

D: I love what you're saying, and I'm getting a little bit overwhelmed already with thinking, "Now, where am I going to find that five hours of time to devote to these steps?" Is that what you mean by, "America isn't ready for tantra"?

M: I think America needs to have more education about ecstatic sexuality because we come from a Judeo-Christian tradition in which the flesh and the spirit are divided and even in opposition. It has been said that the body is the abode of evil instincts and that we have to control it and control our sexual instincts in order to know God. We must begin to realize that it is not like that—that sexuality can be a prayer, it can be felt as a wonderful gesture of love and adoration and awakening. This requires some intense educational efforts. Most people don't have a clue about understanding sexuality in this way.

D: The critique I've heard about tantra is that it's just an excuse for getting off sexually.

M: Yes, this is because America doesn't understand the whole notion of sexuality being sacred. America has sexuality plugged into a dimension of guilt and greed and desire and Playboy magazines and pornography, and this is the result of the eminent guilt and repression of sexual energy, which exists in this Puritanical culture.

But sexual energy can never be repressed because it's at the root of life and the root of creativity. If it weren't for sexual energy, there wouldn't be a single animal, insect, plant, or human being on this planet. So the idea of repressing sexuality and channeling it according to certain acceptable rules is a good and worthy cause, but to repress it is never going to work. You just need to look at what happens to the Catholic priest and the 180 cases of sexual abuse that are currently happening in the Catholic Church, who still doesn't want to include women into the whole equation.

D: So actually, what I'm hearing you say is that sexual energy becomes a vehicle to transport us into the spiritual realms.

M: Yes, you see, it's a very delicate matter. I'm speaking from a high perspective here, I'm not speaking to try to get the common mortal educated about the orgasmic process, because quite frankly, I am so bored with talking about that. I've done it for 20 years. What I'm interested in right now is to teach from the higher perspectives. For those who are beginning, I tell them to go to the people who have trained with me, who are certified SkyDancer teachers—Michael Pooley and Steve and Lokita Carter—and they will tell you all about this.

Yes, sexual energy is a vehicle that transports us to higher levels of consciousness. What comes to mind is a conference I recently attended in which the Dalai Lama, His Holiness, the leader of the Tibetan people, who is now living in India in Dharmsala, and who's a very respected and revered world teacher, was presenting a ritual called The Kalachakra Transmission to 5,000 people or 10,000 people in Toronto. I attended all the Kalachakra transmissions. This was similar to a tantric ritual very close to the kinds of practices and processes I'm teaching—in which it was very clearly plain to people that, yes, do make love, but first of all, choose the right partner. Choose a partner who is in the same lineage as you are, in the same spiritual practice, in the same direction. And make love not because you want to satisfy some greedy need or instinct the way we want to sneeze and relieve ourselves of a pressure or a tension. Make love in a way where you're not attached to the orgasmic release and pluck the energy of pleasure to transform it as a motor or a vehicle to enter into emptiness, which is the very nature of consciousness itself, which is the nature of awakening to the presence of your being.

D: Mmm, yes.

M: That's why at the highest level, the practices that I teach are about the art of disappearing inside each other. This occurs when partners have really known how to tune in with each other, which is an art in itself that requires a body that is at ease and can move and change positions easily. So yoga helps. It also requires the art of breathing; there is orgasmic breathing as opposed to general breathing. Orgasmic breathing is deep and slow and happens through the mouth and goes all the way to the sexual organs. A couple must also master the art of moving together, the art of looking into each other's eyes and connecting soul-to-soul, and the art of letting go, deeply, with each other. It requires trusting in the heart, which is also important. And of course, clear communication.

So all these wonderful skills are things that partners have to hone into. It's an art, it's an education, it's a practice. It doesn't come just like that—once their sexual organs are in contact with each other and they pick up the sensations of that pleasure with the breath and the micro movements—then they can transform love into bliss. And they can disappear beyond the mind into a very vast cosmic consciousness, which allows them to come in touch with their true nature.

D: What I sense, Margot, as I listen to you, is that I have a path with which to use my body to connect to my soul. I love the definition of tantra as 'weaving,' and how well you weave. You teach us all to weave our bodies and our mind and our soul together to create one fabric. You give us these practices with which to navigate our path.

M: Yes, exactly. Well put.

D: Thank you. You're working now on Eight Secrets to a Great Love Life. Will you tell us about that and how these secrets relate to what you've been talking about—all these practices that allow us to transform energy into spirituality.

M: Well, I would say that the first of these eight secrets is The Art of Slowing. This is the ability to let go of the past and to be fully present moment-to-moment to what's happening with your partner. That's the secret of being in the flow. You know how often we have unspoken resentments, blocks in our hearts that we don't want to share, mental interpretations of what our partner does and what it means, all of these things trigger contractions in the heart because it reminds us of our mother or our father or some old wound that we carry.

D: Yes.

M: And so, we don't express these resentments because we're very busy running our daily life, and then we're surprised that after a while, there is no more flow with our sexual energy or our desire. It's often because we are not able to let go of the past. We have accumulated frustrations, unspoken frustrations, and we have forgotten that truth is erotic. When we speak our truth, we take a chance, of course, to be rejected or not to be understood, but if we are communicating with a partner who is in love with us and who is intelligent, then that will be an opportunity for the two partners to grow beyond the predicament that they're in. So, that's why, in a way, truth is erotic, because it's challenging, and it pushes you to grow.

The second secret is Awakening the Wild Self. It teaches that in each of us there is a wild man and wild woman, who actually delight in the power of expressing wildness in a non-aggressive way, or even if it's aggressive, to do it in a playful way. Not to hurt the other, but to do it through laughter, screaming, dancing, jumping, and doing dynamic meditations together. Doing a lot of rock dancing and yelling and gibberish and sounds and pushing each other's shoulders back and forth. There is a tremendous power in this ability that we practice in this way to let loose. It's sort of a preliminary preparation in the ability to let loose in the orgasmic response.

D: It's so interesting because I think we're taught in our daily lives, and especially in our work lives, to do the opposite—to repress, hold in, act professional, act appropriate, etcetera. And so, to have the opportunity to let go and be wild, as you say, sounds wonderful and challenging.

M: Yes, yes, yes. We have a hard time doing this in this culture because there's so much violence associated with sex.

D: Oh, of course.

M: You know whenever someone gets really loose and angry, it's difficult. For example, I just had a wonderful therapy session with my partner. What came up was the whole question of me having chosen to be a bitch and really let loose for three hours at the end of some kind of moment in our lives where there was definitely a hurt on my part, and I was feeling contracted and hurt. Often we express our hurt with a tremendous amount of anger. I, for one, believe according to the French way and the European way, that to really let loose and to allow myself as a woman to be, once in a while, a total bitch, is actually a great way of checking whether my partner has balls and can really stand up to this power.

D: Yes, I see.

M: And so, if you are with a man who is afraid of you—or afraid of his mother, or of the memory of his mother, or just afraid of anger generally because nobody ever raised their voice in his family—if he doesn't know how to deal with your anger or feels too tender, it's not going to work very well. He's going to resent your strength, he's going to run away, he's going to feel upset. But if you have a partner who knows their own power and is able to face you and growl and respond and attack and scream at the same level at which you're doing it—without touching each other, but just for the sheer enjoyment of making noise together—it becomes a tremendous heart opener. You end up doing that with laughter because you've catharted it out.

D: I think it's interesting to note that the sexuality and the anger centers in the brains are situated very close together. So when we get angry, we also can start feeling our sexual and love energy.

M: Yes, that's why, before they make love, when they

get ready to make love, partners often end up having a huge quarrel because their resistances and their armoring, with which they hold themselves tightly together in order to control their daily lives, are softening up. So their wildness comes out, and of course, all the little gremlins and the little demons that are being kept at bay are now having a field day coming out and letting loose. One of my great tantric teachers in India once said, "You cannot be orgasmic in love if you don't know how to be orgasmic in anger."

D: I think it's important, though, to have anger expressed in certain ways. I am not interested in my partner dumping their anger on me as much as I'm interested in their expression of anger. I can really accept that and appreciate that, but I don't want it dumped on me in a blameful, destructive way where he puts me down or....

M: Yes, I agree. I agree, but what I'm saying is, if once in a while, someone has a catharsis where they just lose it and they completely let it out, this can be beneficial. I personally am one, having been an encounter group leader in Germany and Europe for three years, who relishes this kind of purification. It's interesting to know that there are certain populations in the highest Himalayan plateaus—a friend of mine did a film on this—who have this great catharsis among all members of the tribe once a year at the new year. On one end of this divide on this mountain, all the women gather, and on the other end, facing the women with a divide in between, the men gather. And after having drunk a few good drinks, they do this dance with the drums, and they completely attack each other and yell. "Why did you go with this one?" and "Why did you do that?" Everybody lets loose, and they have a huge dance with the drums going and a sort of mock fight. Then after that, they have a celebration.

D: Mmm.

M: That's the thing that in this culture, I feel we have this tortoise shell covering us. We don't know the joyful power of anger, well-released and well-expressed.

D: Well, I think men in the American culture have more permission to get angry. Women have more permission to be sad and hurt. Generally speaking. I have felt that, as a woman, I have lost experience because I've had less opportunity to really get angry in a cathartic, strengthening way. I agree, it's important to do that. When I express anger, I really feel empowered, and yet, with my primary partner, when I have anger, it's scary. There is that fear of, "What will he think and how will he act?"

M: I agree. This can only happen in a very protected and controlled environment. It really can't happen just like that. Part of awakening the wild self is expressing Kali (Kali is the Hindu Goddess of Destruction and Creation), which is something we did in the women's workshop you attended. If you remember, Diana, there was a morning meditation where all the women were invited to freely express the Kali within themselves, which is all the anger of the world that had gathered in their belly, from all the ways that the women of the world are being treated and all the wounds that they have accumulated. In this Kali meditation, the women had a chance to dance it out and to scream it out. Everybody said it was very important for them, and they really loved it. So that kind of ability to awaken the wild self in a way which is non-attacking of the other, but which is simply expressing the delight in the power of wildness, is something that helps us to let loose and to feel okay about it.

D: I agree.

M: That's the second secret. And the third is Laughter, Humor, and Celebration in Love, because we take sexual matters way too seriously. Sex can be a feast. The best orgasms end in laughter. Laughter in itself is a form of orgasmic release. So, we celebrate laughter and humor in the erotic context. We want great lovers to be great clowns.

D: Ahh. That brings up some images.

M: Yes, because you see, when someone really opens up and releases, there is a connection between the sexual center, the belly, and the heart. When that connection really opens, then laughter happens. It's a natural expression of that connection.

D: How blissful.

M: Yes, how blissful, indeed. Also, it's there because it allows us to be in the position of the witness, to kind of delight in the energy and watch it and be in and out of it. So it's wonderful. Then the next secret is Mastering the Power of Love, which is an understanding that there needs to be a balance between power and acceptance. If both lovers are in their power in the right way, that means that they trust themselves and they have a good sense of self-esteem. So whatever the other is doing is not necessarily going to wipe them off the face of the earth. They don't get destroyed if their partner is either attacking or having a hard time or being critical. They know that it's their partner's stuff and that they can keep on going, loving themselves.

And so mastering the power of being, truly standing in the power of who you are, and at the same time having acceptance of the other, is very linked. The more I have a sense of my own power and my own self-acceptance, the more I can also allow myself to accept my partner how they are, and the more I can trust to surrender, which is really letting go in my partners arms without feeling I'm gong to lose my sense of being in charge of myself or of my life. So, it's knowing that we deserve the very best in sexual loving and are prepared to give the best. Also, it requires this deep sense of self-esteem, self-acceptance of who we are, regardless of what the other says or does.

D: It sounds to me in all of this that you're talking so much about how to live our lives as well as how to love sexually. It sounds like there are so many lessons we can learn through studying sexuality and focusing on sexuality, so many lessons we can learn about life itself.

M: Yes, it's very connected, how we accept energy and how we move with it. For instance, one of the other eight secrets is "the Secret of Sexual Connection" and how a deep sexual connection has so much to do with sexual communication. We need to speak to each other during the act of love, before and after, in very, very specific ways that are enhancing the experience and not cutting it off. There are all sorts of little tips and tricks that are wonderful, but that often people don't think about. For instance, if a man is making love to a woman, it's very good for a woman if he asks her before he penetrates, "May I come in and visit?" This allows her to choose whether she's ready to have her body penetrated.

D: Yes.

M: And then it's also very helpful if the man asks her, "Is it okay now if I come?" or "if I have an orgasm?" or "Can I now leave the garden, the sacred garden?" meaning now it's time for him to retire, to leave her body. It's also wonderful for him to close the door after he's left, to take very softly the palm of his hand and lay it on the yoni of the woman. This allows her to get back into her own energy, because she was very open and filled up by someone else, and now she needs to find herself again. These are little things that seem like nothing, but they make the entire difference for a woman between a clumsy lover and a great lover.

D: Well, I think you're talking about the power of ritual.

So often I think people don't understand what ritual is, but I know you have placed a huge focus on ritual, because it focuses energy and creates a safe and sacred space. Wouldn't you say?

M: Oh yes. Absolutely. Rituals are basically—energetically—ways of creating mandalas of energy, of creating the four corners of the room, of calling the four directions, of calling the protectors, and of basically allowing the mind to quiet itself down because it knows that now we are entering into a realm in which the soul, the energy, and the breath are primordial. And so, rituals help us to focus, they help us to open our third eye between the two eyebrows, which is the center of vision. They help us to have a clear direction as to where we're going together. They help us to feel safe, also, in opening up deeper.

D: I love how you explain things in a way that makes so much sense and that actually makes me want to learn more about this.

M: Good, wonderful!

D: Yes. So, you have four more secrets for couples. Do you want to share them with us now?

M: Well, I can say that the other secrets are awakening your orgasmic response together, how to stimulate each other to great orgasm, erotic devotion, and how to heal—that's very important, how to heal old wounds so we can flow with our energies. Those are some of the secrets I haven't talked about yet tonight, but they're important.

D: Oh, excellent. Margot, there's one more question I'd like to ask you: if you had a message to give our readers, people who are living their ordinary lives and living and loving as best they can, what would you say to them?

M: I would say that it's very important today in the world that we live in to have impeccable lives. To bring ourselves to focus on being an impeccable person in the way that we deal with each other. One of the most important things for me in my love life is to truly be able to have respect for my partner, to admire the way they behave, and to know that I can count on them, that they are there for me and I'm there for them.

I find today that we have to remember that when we as women heal ourselves or do work on ourselves, we don't just do it for ourselves, but we do it for all the women in the world. And when men work on their healing, they don't do it just for themselves, but they do it for all the men in the world. This is so important because right now there is a deep, deep oppression of women in the world. I just read an article on sexual slavery, and I was appalled to find out that there are one million young beings who are traded every year for sexual slavery, and it starts at the age of four years old.

D: Oh, my goodness.

M: Toddlers who are four years old and up are traded to be used as sexual toys and then discarded once they've caught AIDs. It's very, very bad, and so we need to be really conscious about the way we practice our sexuality, to really do it in as pure and loving a way as possible. Men need to be able to listen to women, to awaken their inner feminine, to understand the flowing art of the woman. And women need to understand the strength of the masculine within themselves and how it can protect them as women. When the yin and the yang (Yin and Yang are Chinese words for feminine and masculine energy) are awake in each of us, then we have a chance to move through our wounds and our difficulties more easily, I would say.

D: Well, I think you are doing such a wonderful service to all of us, teaching us to balance that energy of yin and yang, male and female, and to create more peace in our world. I thank you for your work, and I thank you for your time.

M: Thank you, it's been a pleasure.

D: And Margo, before we go, will you tell us how we can reach you and where we can learn more about your work and your upcoming teaching programs?

M: You can go to www.margotanand.com or to the Institute of Ecstatic Living at www.estaticliving.com.

D: Wonderful, and again, it has been a tremendous pleasure to speak with you today.

M: Thank you so very much. Thank you, it was fantastic to talk with you. It was really a delight to be talking to a sister.

D: Thank you, Margot.

Interview Commentary with Diana and Bill

Bill: I really enjoyed your interview with Margot. What was particularly interesting to me, Diana, was how she talked about the meaning of tantra and how it's really a joining of the spirit and the body. When I think about tantra practice, I recall that Tibetan tantra includes concentration and eye gazing and so forth, but I think she's specifically talking about sexual union here. So I'm wondering what your reaction was to the way Margot defined tantra.

Diana: Well, I loved her description. It was very poetic, especially where she talks about choosing with awareness what brings us pleasure. That's what makes our soul sing. I think actually she's talking about how we can use sexuality as a gateway to spirituality. I've participated in another workshop with Margot since you and I had that interview with her. I can really speak from personal experience how the sexual centers of our body have very strong energy. The tantric masters would have expressed it as dense energy. Yes, dense energy as opposed to the finer and higher vibrations of the upper level chakras.

B: Do you mean the heart chakra or some of the other chakras in the head?

D: Yes, the heart is the bridge between the upper and lower chakras. The upper chakras are the throat center, third eye center (in the middle of the forehead) and the crown chakra center (at the top of the head).

The throat is connected to the quality of communication and creativity. The third eye center is connected to inner wisdom and intuition. The crown center connects us to divinity in ourselves and in all of life. It helps us feel oneness with all that is. When people are opened in the crown center, they report seeing and feeling light, love, bliss and unity with the ALL.

The 1st chakra is located at the base of the spine and the pelvic floor. It's connected with the genitals and uterus. It's function is survival and reproduction. It's power is to feel emotions and sensations (including orgasm). The 2nd chakra is located in the belly in the area of the navel. It's connected to the womb, hips and lower back. It's function is to flow with life to express emotions and to bring us strength and health. The 3rd chakra is located in the rib cage down to the navel. It also includes the lower and middle spine. It is associated with personal power and a sense of identity and independence.

As one can see, the energies of the first three chakras are very strong. They are connected to the earth, our survival instincts and to power. It's no wonder that bringing these energies up to the heart intensifies the experience of loving tremendously. In the tantra tradition, we continue bringing these energies up to the throat chakra and intensify this through making sounds, talking, laughing, moaning or screaming in ecstasy. To continue transforming this energy, we bring it up to the 6th and 7th chakras.

I experienced this process myself. I brought my sexual energy up to my third eye, and I felt an expanded sense of peace, bliss and pleasure that is what Margot calls a 'full-body orgasm.'

B: So you had actually had that experience.

D: Yes. I really understand what Margot means when she talks about the full-body orgasm that is a blend of sexual and spiritual energy. I felt very blissed out and very open and spacious and peaceful in a much fuller way than I would have with just — and I say 'just' — a genital orgasm. Genital orgasms are wonderful. They're very intensely pleasureful for most of us. At the same time, this type of full-body orgasm lasts much longer and is intensely pleasureful throughout the body. It is heart-opening and connecting to all of life. It's like I'm floating in the cosmos, seeing shooting stars all around me, feeling the ecstasy of beauty and love in me and in life.

B: Wonderful. Here's a question that came up for me when I was listening to you and Margot talk: you know, it's easy for us, those of us who are spiritual seekers to understand this connection between the spirit and the body, but I just wonder for someone who's new to this area, is that going to be easy for someone to work with, to bring the spiritual dimension into their sex life?

D: Well, that's a good question. Will it be easy? The thing that I like about it is it gives people permission to open up. Actually Margot said it so well when she talked about the Judeo-Christian tradition that defines the body as wrong and bad and less worthy, less important, less meaningful than the soul. So we've been taught to deny the body and go to the mind and go to the heavens for our spiritual connection. Tantra teachers like Margot and the tantric masters focus on the body as the gateway to the soul. I, as a tantric practitioner, only need to open to my heart and listen to my body, and breathe, practicing the four keys to an orgasmic experience: breath, movement, sound and presence.

As I breathe deeply and focus my attention on my pelvis—the first chakra—I intensify the sexual pleasure I'm experiencing. Instead of releasing it through a genital orgasm, I intentionally focus on bringing the energy up to my heart, letting the strength of it intensify my experience of loving my partner and myself. I continue breathing and intentionally bring the sexual and love energy up to my third eye—the sixth chakra—and then above my head—the seventh chakra. In doing this, the strong sexual energy and pleasure intensifies the experience of connection with my partner, with the divine and with all of life.

The invitation is there for everyone to explore and to experiment with what is uniquely pleasureful for them, so that they don't have to deny the body in order to be spiritual, in order to feel good and to feel loving. The loving comes in loving myself first. The way I do that is to define myself as my own Beloved — to make love to myself, so to speak. I do this by finding ways to pleasure myself, filling myself up with love emotionally and with pleasure physically. And from that place of fullness, I have so much to give to others. The next step is to see the Beloved in my partner. If I don't have a primary partner, then to really look for the Beloved in each person's eyes that I meet throughout the day and each experience I have, so that my heart stays open, and my intent is to love in whatever way I can, which is what spirituality is all about. It's about loving.

This practice is especially helpful to bridge the differences between men and women. As a sex therapist, I have heard many women complain about their partners only being interested in sex. The complaints center around sex being mechanical, automatic, impersonal, too fast, too rough. Women tend to feel used and taken for granted if men don't bring a tender, loving and sensitive attitude to lovemaking. Many women tell me that they cry silently after sex while their partners are sound asleep beside them. They then withdraw emotionally and try to avoid sex as much as possible. They become mechanical in their lovemaking too because they think that they can't get their emotional or physical needs met. This creates a stalemate in which both partners stop communicating and sex becomes dull and boring.

B. That brings me to the next response I had to your interview, which is: are Americans ready for this? Is there a place for tantra in American life with this heavy, Judeo-Christian background division of spirit and body? I mean this is pioneering work. You're very involved with it — how do you feel about that? What's your comfort level around that?

D: I'd like to start by saying that several of my friends have been critical of workshops where there is the possibility of nudity or intimate touching or discussion of personal issues involving sexuality. They believe that the area of sexuality should be relegated to one's own bedroom and not shared with anyone. This is a common point of view, I think, that perpetuates dysfunction, misinformation, misunderstandings between people and a lot of pain.

When we want to learn about something, we usually take classes. This includes learning life skills. There are classes these days in high school about child care. The teenagers are given computerized baby dolls that they are required to care for and take responsibility for constantly, as if they were real babies with real needs. The students learn through experience how serious and difficult child rearing is and are much better able to make informed decisions about marriage and pregnancy.

Even though our society is rampant with sexually explicit advertising, movies, television shows, news stories and pornography, we tend not to support learning about sexuality in any way except through books. I wouldn't have gone to tantra workshops myself except that I thought I could learn much valuable information to share with clients. What I didn't realize was that sexuality is so personal and so connected to my ability to express love that when I started exploring sexual experiences in a group, it brought up inhibitions, blocks, low self-esteem, self doubt, distrust and other feelings that I had denied and repressed. I grew emotionally and spiritually in ways I never have in the 61 years I've lived. And I experienced others doing the same thing.

I still believe that learning about sexuality is very simple. It is based on the PLISSIT model developed by Jack Annon I learned in sex therapy many years ago. (See diagram on page 204.)

Permission Giving: Most people who have issues with sexuality learn through receiving permission to be sexual and to express their sexuality in their own unique way. I remember the experience in the sexuality workshop for women over forty. Margot asked us who liked sex more after menopause. Half of the women raised their hands. They felt validated through the support of others like them in the room to really enjoy their sexuality. Margot then asked who liked sex less after menopause. Again, half the women in the room responded. Suddenly, these women felt support. They, too, received permission to have their own experience. It was no longer embarrassing or shameful to admit it. From this place of awareness to acceptance, they had more informed choices of what to do about their feelings. (See diagram on page 205.)

Limited Information: I remember our discussion of the varieties of orgasmic and non-orgasmic experiences that women had and what it took to have an orgasm. Women learned from each other how to heighten their own pleasure and how to deepen their experience of orgasm or what to do to renew their interest in sex and orgasm after menopause.

Specific Suggestions: Men's experience of learning about how to facilitate women having a multi-orgasmic experience was interesting. They were given specific suggestions about how to stimulate the women, and the women were taught how to communicate in detail what was pleasurable to them. They were then instructed to communicate clearly to their partners where and how they could be touched to enhance their pleasure. Everyone was amazed at the depth of pleasure women received when these specific suggestions were followed.

Intense Therapy: There were usually several people in our workshops who were very unhappy. Even with all of the support and information in thee workshops, it was obvious they would need more intense work with a therapist or sexuality coach. One couple was struggling because she was interested in exploring her sexuality outside of their marriage. Her husband was very much against this idea. Therapy was recommended for them to resolve their conflict.

Margot has talked about the issue of time and goal-orientation that Americans have. The issue of time is a big one because we split and scatter ourselves in so many ways. So to take time for ourselves, our partners, our families, is a blessing. It's like blessing ourselves with the willingness to be who we are and relax into the experience of taking time with each other and with ourselves. And that's what intimacy is. Intimacy (in-to-me-you-see) is the courage to be ourselves. Yes, I think it's a stretch; it's a challenge.

What I've found in the workshops I've participated in is that taking this time is a vehicle to ecstatic and blissful living. The minute I start taking time my energy starts relaxing and I start claiming that energy for myself instead of dispersing it. Actually, the tantra way of breathing is to build up energy and in high states of arousal to learn how to relax. We can apply that to our everyday lives. In high states of activity, high states of work and intensity, we can learn how to relax and love who we are and where we are in the moment. To cultivate our awareness, we need to develop the ability to witness our experience, and from that place we can always choose to love. This is a challenge, yet it's a wonderful way of coming back home to the ecstasy and bliss that is available to us in every moment.

B: It's as though the average person works all day, he comes home from work, he put his feet up, has a beer, watches TV, falls asleep, gets up in the morning, and goes back to work. What you're implying with your comments here, Diana, is that in fact, if he would come home and focus on these practices, every night that he's home watching a football game or having dinner with his family, he could be in ecstasy. That's the big secret. That's the big secret of tantra: ecstasy is actually available in his own body, with his own wife, with his own sweetheart, with his own Beloved.

D: That's true. The thing with being in ecstasy while watching TV would be quite a trick because tantra invites people to really focus in on the breath, the movement and the sound, the energy of life that's flowing both in myself as well as in my partner. There's a lot around eye gazing and connection, bringing our focus, our attention to the present moment, staying aware. So often with TV or with other activities that we either go into a trance or expect that relaxing means somehow becoming unconscious.

B: Yes, life as a spectator sport.

D: Yes, or life as if we're just going through the motions: we've done our work all day and now we can rest, and resting means tuning out.

B: And being dull, being dulled.

D: Yes. Tantra and the tantric lifestyle is all about waking up to the present moment and the mystery of life that is contained in each moment. When I wake up and open to the moment as my Beloved partner, I become alive and expressive.

B: So it's all about being alive; it's all about aliveness.

D: Yes, it's about waking up. There's a lot of risk-taking, I think, in letting go of the future and of the past, and of staying right in the moment. Because in the moment, there is no control, but there is total opportunity to be here, fully, and there's everything we need for our own wholeness, our own happiness in the present moment. But the ego gets very attached to thinking that we should plan and be in control of everything in order to be happy. But it's not true; it's a story we've been taught and have continued to tell ourselves.

B: When I hear you and Margot speak — and I've heard other SkyDancing teachers speak□— my reaction is, I could actually keep, develop and deepen the best feelings that I've ever had when I first fell in love with somebody. That magical time when you're completely engrossed in the other person. It sounds to me like this tantric lifestyle can actually cultivate love to where it's even beyond that initial infatuation. You can actually explore these realms fully as a participant with total aliveness.

D: I love your thoughts on this, Bill, and I would go further to say that Margot does an inner lover guided imagery that I have found exquisite. She actually asks people — and I would encourage our readers to do this while I speak about it — asks people to think of the highlights of times in their lives when they felt fully loved. And just go through them one at a time and deeply immerse themselves in the feeling of being loved and of loving someone. So that in doing that, I then heighten my experience of love. From there, pick out one particular memory or experience that really feels particularly exciting and attractive and step into it. Actually revisit it and experience that feeling of being loved and loving. From there imagine that you become both the giver and the receiver, that you are actually making love to yourself the way you have been made love to or the way you have been offered love. It could be from your child or your pet or a wonderful experience of a sunset. So it's not that you would have to have the perfect lover in order to do this exercise. The idea is to feel that nurturing, that blessing of feeling love and step into that place of giving that to yourself. And then from that place, look at your life now and examine when and how you can give that to yourself today. You take it into the experience of the present, and ask "how can I bless myself with love today and how can I create a spiritual practice of this every day?"

B: Now is this one of those eight secrets that you and Margot were talking about?

D: Actually, she does have that as number three, mastering the power of love. The one I was really interested in talking about with you, is the second secret, awakening the wild self. I thought it was very interesting because to me it feels very counter to the ways that we have been taught to act in our society. Margot really encourages all of us to go full into the wild energy of passion and anger and express ourselves totally and fully. I said to her on the interview itself that that's very counter to how we've been taught. But I also know that when I've done that in the workshops as well as in my personal life, I really do tune in to my own personal power and the universal power that I can tap into in life.

I suggest that people express their anger constructively. There's a particular model that is based on the 3 stages of anger. The 1st stage is the fiery stage of anger where our energy for fighting and striking out at the other is very strong. The 2nd stage is communicating constructively and sharing your needs. The 3rd stage is making up. This is a time for cuddling and holding each other, and re-establishing the closeness that was lost. (For a detailed description of this process, see the section titled "Expressing Anger Constructively" at the end of this book).

What about you, Bill?

B: I love the fact that you mentioned that the anger center and the sex center are very close to each other in the brain. As a scientist I found that fascinating because that's been my experience. We know that couples sometimes have a big fight, and then they have fabulous sex. Some therapists say that's really bad because that's make-up sex, you know. You're a psychotherapist, what's your reaction to all that and the connection between those two places?

D: I've seen that happen, as have you, time and again, where people have an argument and then they make up in a very passionate way because they've been very stimulated and aroused and empowered through their expression of anger. However, as we talked about in the interview itself, people get afraid of anger. They fear anger as well as orgasm and passion. No wonder people tend to want to repress anger and also passion. I understand that orgasm is the ultimate letting go besides death. In fact, the word orgasm in French means 'little death'.

A very juicy and thought-provoking question to consider is what's that fine line between being aggressive and hurting another person and giving myself full permission to be passionate and express my anger juicily, openly and in an enlivening way where I may yell or stamp my feet or pound my pillow. What are peoples' experiences with that? With me, the fine line is, I put a stop to anything that feels disrespectful to me. If a person is expressing their anger, I'm really rooting for them. I support that totally; and if it starts getting personal, directed towards me, in a disrespectful or downgrading way, then I would stop it, even if that means leaving the situation.

B: So what you're saying is similar to what I learned in conflict resolution classes. You can express your anger and you can feel your anger as long as you're not shaming and blaming the other person that's involved in the process.

D: Exactly. We do a little exercise called 'Lion's Play' at the beginning of many of our tantric sharing experiences. The Lion's Play is simply that place where we get playfully physical with each other, where we'll growl and we'll push each other and we'll wrestle and toss and turn on the ground and really use as full force as possible to push and actually feel our power. That's the idea — to feel our power and feel that contact with our partner in that place of being empowered and being fully present with our life energy and expressing that fully to our partner. Wow, is that an impassioned experience, where it really raises the energy of passion and excitement and power and strength.

B: I'm getting kind of excited just talking about it.

D: [laughter] Thank you Bill, it was wonderful talking with you, as usual.

Chapter 5:

Relationship as a Spiritual Path

A conversation with Diana Owens about emotional intimacy, truth as a turn on, and honoring our partner's needs as well as our own.

Bill: This series of interviews focuses on sexuality and spirituality, and particularly, relationship as a spiritual path. To begin with, Diana, why don't you tell us a little bit about that? What are we about to investigate?

Diana: This is my favorite topic, Bill. It's what I live, and I'm inviting all of our readers to live this, too. Relationship as a spiritual path means that we use life as our primary partner. Through this experience of living life, we recognize that every moment is a moment of intimacy. Intimacy is the courage to be myself. When I experience life intimately, I take any experience as a mirror and a reflection of who I am in the present moment. If I don't like what's happening, I can take responsibility for changing the situation or myself or both. This allows for much growth.

B: It's interesting that you're talking first about relationship to yourself. I'm curious how sexuality relates. What does sex have to do with this?

D. At the deepest level, sex is about loving. And loving is a way for each of us to open up to ourselves and to our partner, to connect from our heart. In this place of openness and connection, we experience more fully our own aliveness and essential nature. There's a teaching in the field of spirituality and sexuality that says that if we didn't have the right and the responsibility to use our bodies for pleasure, we wouldn't have been given bodies capable of pleasure. The body is our vehicle of communication, of self-expression. I talk a lot about body wisdom, or body truth, when I'm working with my clients.

B: Are we still getting over the Puritanical influence in our culture? It seems to me that the Europeans are much freer and more open about sexuality than we are in America.

D: Well, as a sex therapist and a coach in sexuality and spirituality, I've given presentations to college age students. And I ask the question, "How many of you have been given the affirmation and the permission from your parents to go out and enjoy sex and have a good time?" And, usually, about three out of twenty people raise their hands. So the answer is, "Yes, we are still getting over it." The primary institutions that influence us about our sexuality are the family and the church. And they're the slowest to change. That's why most kids get their information about sexuality from their peers and from the media, rather than from their parents. The church plays a large role in creating inhibitions and negativity in people about sexuality.

B: When I was a teenager, I had a young woman friend who had just come out of Catholic school. She said that the nuns told her that if she sat in a boy's lap, she'd get pregnant.

D: Yes, well, I could tell you lots of other stories about that, too. There are a number of different churches that have banned sex for those who are not married. People in our society have not been given permission to be sexual. And yet sexuality is present from birth to death. Did you know that newborn male babies have erections 50% of the time before the umbilical cord is cut? And baby girls will have a vaginal discharge much of the time at birth.

B: No, I didn't know that at all.

D: Every 90 minutes of our lives, men have mini- or major-erections and women lubricate vaginally. So we are sexual beings from womb to tomb, so to speak. And yet we aren't really given either permission or appreciation of ourselves as sexual beings. Where spirituality plays into this is that spirituality is about the meaning of life and oneness with all that is, the essence of life. And the essence of life, as I see it, is loving. We can say that sexuality is our capacity to love fully. Now, we don't always define it that way or give it that meaning, but the full sense of sexuality is heightening our ability to express ourselves fully and lovingly moment to moment. As we do this, we start identifying the blocks to our loving, wounds we have that influence us to close down or numb out. This becomes a spiritual path where we have the opportunity again and again to choose to continue to open up and love. This is the heightening of consciousness that is what spirituality is. We all have this capacity and can live intimately every moment through this process.

B: That's a very inspiring perspective, Diana. And what I'm hearing is that the spiritual path of relationship applies not only to having a primary partner with whom we're intimate, but also to cultivating an intimacy with all of life and with ourselves.

D: Yes, very well said. We begin by opening to ourselves and our own inner experience. We cultivate the strength to accept all that we are with our light and our shadow, opening to loving ourselves fully with awareness. This brings us the pleasure of being who we are in the present moment and the ecstasy of knowing this is all there is and this is enough. This pleasure and bliss is reflected in high levels of energy physically emotionally and spiritually. We can then expand this capacity to be in the moment with love enjoying sharing who we are honestly, openly and ecstatically with a partner. When we engage in this way with another person, we are increasing our own pleasure; we're also enhancing their pleasure, and in the sharing of this, the heart opens more and more fully, heightening our consciousness and expanding our awareness of being.

B: Well, let's talk a little more about the shared sexual experience, specifically, what turns men on and what turns women on. And I'm curious about something that perhaps you would begin by commenting on. When I was in junior high school, my biology teacher once said that men are stimulated visually because the visual sense is the strongest sense. And so for the species to procreate, it's very important, if men are initiators, to look at a woman's body and get aroused. What do you think of that idea?

D: I think you're right, that particular statistic is certainly well known—that men respond visually. Another research finding is that men are strongly aroused by the physicality of lovemaking. So, in addition to the visual, they love the action, the movement, of intercourse. They love the action of sexual stimulation—both giving sexual stimulation as well as receiving it. By the way, giving pleasure to his partner through sexual stimulation is just as much a turn on to a man as it is for him to receive sexual stimulation.

B: I would agree with that. That's certainly my experience. It's very satisfying for me to turn a woman on.

D: So often, unfortunately, men feel a lot of pressure to perform. That appears to be a deep source of pain and anxiety for a man. Men often elevate the importance of erection and orgasm in lovemaking above the loving connection. This has become the age of Viagra, where we have the magic pill, so to speak, to allow a man this experience of arousal and pleasure. But even with Viagra, men still feel a lot of pressure to perform, at least the men I've talked to and worked with. They say they feel like failures if they have to take Viagra.

B: I have seen that men have been taught—partly through women's liberation—that it's very important to help a woman achieve orgasm. The idea about the sacredness of the clitoris and how some women don't get clitoral stimulation in penetration, took a whole generation of men, gave them pause, and said, "Oh, there are other things I need to do to satisfy my woman." Would you talk about that a little bit?

D: It's so interesting, those last words you said, about what I need to do to satisfy my woman. Don't you hear expectations in that, Bill?

B: Oh yea.

D: And so, how do you as a man feel about those expectations?

B: Well, I think that being testosterone-type beings, we're naturally into performance. When you said men are into the action of sex, I would have to agree with that as a man. That aspect of lovemaking can be fascinating to me. But the inner, deeper, feminine components of connection and merging have been of even more interest to me. So that's been an area of great growth for me, to bring my heart into my sexual experience.

D: Mmm, that's so beautiful, Bill. Many men have fear of connecting and opening to the heart, and, as I was saying earlier, they have fear of under-performing. In fact, one of the biggest inhibitions for both men and women in sexuality is fear. And fear comes from expectations. For this reason, it's so important that each gender knows that they are not responsible for their partner's happiness, pleasure, orgasm, or experience. This isn't easy to accept. When I tell people this, it really takes them off the hook. Some get a little bit guilty and doubtful because they start asking themselves, "How can I relate if I'm not responsible for my partner's happiness?" The truth is that we're each responsible for our own happiness and pleasure, as I take responsibility for my own happiness, I have so much more to give my partner from a place of freedom, spontaneity, and love. Coming from a place of self responsibility allows me to be whole and complete in relating to you, and ask you how I can please you without feeling like I'm having to do it right in order to be a success.

B: So, this practice that some men now have of, "Get the woman off first, then worry about your own orgasm"— you're not particularly recommending that?

D: Actually, I see sexuality as a process and not a goal. That's, again, part of sexuality as a spiritual path—that every moment of a sexual experience is important. Just think of what we can give our partner by being totally in our bodies and at the same time totally soul-oriented. My friend and I

were talking about those two experiences in lovemaking—
that there is this place of being in technique. Have you ever
experienced that, Bill, where you feel like you are wanting to
show off by expressing a certain technique?

B: I'll tell you when that happens to me. If I'm doing
something and the woman is saying, "Oh, that's yummy. Don't
stop," Then I think I've found a good technique with her.
[Laughter] But if I was loving just as much a moment ago and
she wasn't saying that, then I might be looking for that way of
touching her that would be a good technique. And I agree, I
can be taken out of my process that way; I can be removed
from the moment when I'm focusing too much on finding how
to please her.

D: It's interesting to hear about this from your male
perspective. My perspective is a bit different. When you talk
about a woman enjoying what you're doing and saying, "Do
that more, don't stop," what I see as meaningful is the
happiness, pleasure, connection, and love that a woman is
experiencing and expressing through her appreciating what
you're doing. So it's not so much, really, what the man is
doing as much as the connection between the two people
that I see as important. And that experience of pleasure may
change in the very next minute. It seems to me that if a man
is attached to the technique, he's going to miss the person,
he misses the soul of sex. The soul of sex is experienced
when he is really with the person he's making love to, when
he focuses on being with her and moving every step of the
way with her to that next level of pleasure rather than merely
getting her off.

B: So even though there are all these workshops that
teach techniques, all these how-to books on sexual positions,
and so many women's magazines that are filled with
techniques, what you're saying is, it's always going to have a

tendency to take you out of the process and more into being goal-oriented. What I'm hearing you say, Diana, is, "Hey, that woman may be responding to what you're doing, but it may have much less to do with the movements or the pressure or how much tongue or how much teeth; it actually might have everything to do with the experience she's having with you in the moment."

D: Exactly. And even though tantra often teaches technique, it emphasizes that there is no goal in lovemaking. Technique is taught as a means to experience soul-oriented sex, which is about wholeness, about heightened pleasure that can offer transformation to a person and to a couple—where people actually come out of themselves and into the moment of connection, of wholeness, of bliss. So, yes, it's not about technique, it's about listening to myself and you and this moment, and opening to the gigantic possibility of being here now, with each other, loving and opening.

And it's not always pretty, Bill, because when I'm really open with my heart, I open up to the shadow part of myself, as well as the love and the pleasure and the ecstasy. So I might start accessing fear when I get so open and loving. Many of us may never feel safe to open our heart to a lover until we have a committed and trusting relationship. Lovemaking unearths our deepest, most vulnerable self. It can be incredibly intimidating. It's actually the most vulnerable way that we relate as human beings. So when we take our clothes off, it's as though we take our masks off and let our partner see us not just nude, but soulfully, warts and all, so to speak. So that can bring up a lot of fears, a lot of inadequacies, a lot of doubts about, "If this is who I am, and this is what I'm offering, what if you don't like it? It's all I have to give."

B: Well, isn't it true that we are the only mammals that have sex not just for procreation, but for pleasure?

D: Well, I love how wise you are, Bill. I would agree with that statement. And I would add that sex actually has many different facets for human beings. Sex can be approached in a very heightened, elevated way, when two people are expressing love very purely and fully. But sex can also be used, as we all know, in a very negative, painful, or hurtful way. I work a lot with sexual abuse and the effects of rape. There has been an astonishing amount of violent sexual expression in our culture. You see this on the internet these days, with the great number of pornography sites, and in the rape statistics every year. Sex can actually put people in a trance, it can be used to hurt or control someone, and it can take people to the experience of transformation and divine union. So sex, as well as anything else for that matter, is based on the meaning it has for people.

B: So it's really, then, a search for meaning. If you're searching for sexual satisfaction, perhaps one place to look is in the meaning sex has for you. I guess that brings us back to relationship as a spiritual path.

D: That's right. I like you coming back to that. I was thinking about that myself, that as we develop relationship with a primary partner, so often we start asking ourselves a question: "Is this all there is?" And we ask this about sex as well as about the relationship as a whole. I think most of us need far more than simply getting off with our partner in order to feel satisfied and fulfilled. Sex, by itself—in terms of genital sex and having orgasm—can happen so quickly. Seven to fifteen minutes is one of the average statistics for how long people have sex: about fifteen minutes a time, twice a week.

If that's all there is, a lot of people leave that experience feeling very unfulfilled. Well, then, if this is the case, what else is there? I would say that every person needs to ask and answer this question for themselves. What makes sex meaningful to you? What is fulfilling sex? What contributes to you having a meaningful, bliss-filled experience with sex? The way I would address these questions is in what I call the four T's: trust, talk, touch, and time.

Meaningful, fulfilled sex starts with trust—without trust, we don't open to each other. It's very hard to open our hearts, very scary, because we worry about not having acceptance. That comes, so much of the time, from not accepting ourselves. And even though we do not accept ourselves, we do look for that acceptance in another person—that appreciation, affirmation, and veneration, if you want to look at it that way. Appreciating our partner verbally and through our actions creates a sense of acceptance, which builds trust. So does keeping agreements. If I don't keep an agreement with my partner, I'm not going to build trust. Another way to develop trust is to communicate our conditions for good sex. When I share with my partner my conditions for good sex, and my partner responds, I feel a basic trust that I will be honored and that I will enjoy our sexual experiences together.

B: Well, I'm reminded of Margot Anand's first book, where she says, "People don't take enough time for any kind of sex magic to unfold." And she used to recommend, I think, setting aside one evening to spend four hours with your partner, with the intention of the possibility of a sexual or tantric encounter. And who knows what happens? No expectations, but that much time.

D: Well, I like the practice of time set aside. I strongly recommend that to couples. Actually, because I'm single right now and not in a committed relationship, I take that time for myself. And I encourage people who are single to do the same thing: to really create a ritual of love, where they can look forward to taking time to nurture and nourish who they are through special pleasuring and prayerful experiences that allow them to feel filled with love. The time taken can become a ritual, and people can use that time in whatever way that brings them closer together in pleasure, whether they're with a partner or not.

One of the things we do in the Sacred Sexuality workshops that I offer is a little ritual of sharing. We begin with eye gazing, holding hands, sharing my appreciation for my partner, and hearing their appreciation for me. Then from that place, we create a sacred space where I bless my partner with my intention to be here fully with them, and where I invite them to be fully here with me. From that place of intention, we each talk about what fears we might have and what boundaries we would set—so that I am always coming back to myself and who I am and what works for me, and then I invite my partner to do the same. What happens in this process is a truth telling that opens me up and helps me connect with my partner in a heart-felt way. This sets the scene for lovemaking that comes from the heart and not just from the body.

B: You had begun talking about the four T's. The first was trust. What were the others again?

D: Time, talk, and touch. You and I were talking about how important taking time is. So often, as people spend a lot of time together over many years and get more used to each other, they lose sight of what's really important: that special couple time. When this happens, there's often a lot of grieving and loss that is felt. One or both people start resenting not having that time, and they may feel that they're not very important to the other person. And they lose their juice, some of the life in their partnership is lost. So, not only is it important to make time—I liked what you said before about the four hours of time—but I suggest that people create erotic surprises.

B: Erotic surprises?

D: Yes, for each other. And have erotic dates, where they each make a list of what is particularly erotic for them. Then they give their lists to each other, and each person creates an erotic surprise, once a week or so, as a way of bringing the juice back into the relationship.

B: And that's based on the information the other partner has supplied.

D: Exactly.

B: So if black jockey shorts turned you on, then that's what I would wear.

D: That's right. As a surprise. I'd never know when this would happen or if this would happen. I would dream about it and hope for it, but if one day you appeared in black jockey shorts—if that was my erotic wish and turn on—then I would really be excited, because you were giving me the gift of yourself. I can ask, but when you choose to meet me in that place of my desire, it's the ultimate gift to me.

B: And that's probably why having sex with a partner is usually considered to be more exciting than having sex with yourself, just because there's a tremendous amount of pleasure in pleasing someone, in getting someone excited. So I'm appearing to you in this black underwear, and because it arouses you, then I feel good about that. So it's an exciting experience for me, and I feel more attractive, more seen, more juicy.

D: Exactly. And people hesitate sometimes—a lot of times, really—to tell each other what they really like and what really turns them on. Yet when they do that, it's quite a blessing and a gift to the other one, because the other then knows even more specifically how to please them. And if we're in an intimate relationship, we really do want to please. It's not that I'm making you, as my partner, do something when I tell you what I want. I'm simply letting you get to know who I am. And from that place of your understanding what pleases me, you then can choose to please me in that way or not. I think the important thing is that you have that option, and that I—through my requests—don't make those into requirements; that I don't expect you to do what I ask you to do, but I allow you and invite you to share who I am through that process. At the same time, I give you acceptance if you don't choose to meet those particular requests that I have.

B: And the third T is talk. Tell us about this.

D: Everyone talks about how important communication is in relationships. And communication, when it comes from the soul, is so essential. It is essential to intimacy and understanding; it's also opening to the mind and heart. When I'm truthful with anyone, I'm giving them the gift of myself. I'm also developing emotional and spiritual muscles by being honest, because sometimes it's hard to tell the truth, especially when what I have to say isn't particularly something I think you want to hear. When I'm willing to say it anyway, I invite connection rather than deny it. I invite you into my private world.

That's a gift, and it needs to be received as such. So we take time to communicate about the little things, the big things, the things we might want to leave unsaid. An exercise I've done and that I offer people is a 'Tell Me Who You Are' exercise, where I sit with my Beloved and simply ask him, "Tell me who you are," and then open my heart to listen and receive what he has to say. Eye gazing is an important part of this exercise, so that we see and feel seen. This can be done every day, each partner sharing, and it doesn't need to be for a long time, even five minutes is good. It's a very, very connecting practice.

B: The Sufis call that practice the Daily Devotion.

D: How wonderful. I love that name. In tantra, there's no particular name for it, but the meaning of the word 'tantra'—which is 'to weave'—captures it well. This practice of taking time to be with each other is all about weaving the whole of who we are into our relationship: not just sticking with what's pretty and what's nice, but allowing who I am to be connecting to who you are. When we become willing to learn from that process, to continue to open and to accept, then those qualities of openness and acceptance infuse our relationship. So, yes, talk is vital!

B: And touch?

D: As people live their busy lives, touching is so often forgotten. So, another practice I suggest is to make dates for touching, times when we are together just to touch. It's also important to be open to all kinds of touching, not just a narrow spectrum, and to touch with no goal in mind. I think that's where soul-centered sex comes in. It's not about technique or touching for the sake of getting off, but touching throughout the day, touching as we pass by. Even sexual touching—when my partner fondling my breasts or when I squeeze my partner's buns—is included even though we don't take it further. It's part of our intimate way of saying, "I love you" throughout the day. And if that's not okay, then we need to look at what that's about with an attitude that's curious instead of resentful. So here, it's vital to talk, to take time to get to know one another and what kind of touching is okay, what's not, and why.

B: Well, it seems that sort of thing often happens in the beginning of a relationship, and then it tends to wane.

D: Yes, that's true. So, we really want to examine, "How can we keep that fire burning?"

B: As a sex therapist, that's one of your jobs, right? To keep the fire burning.

D: No, Bill. I never take that on. That's not my job, it's whoever's job is wanting that fire to keep burning. So it's their responsibility. I simply provide a light and offer that light to each person to keep their own fire burning.

B: Well thanks for setting me straight. [Laughter]

D: Any time, Bill.

B: Okay, now we've talked about what turns men on. Let's talk about what turns women on.

D: First of all, I do think that we are all unique, and so there is no pat answer to that question. But my experience has been that what turns women on is love. So often we can get deep into the gender differences and the stereotypes that what turns men on is sex while what turns women on is love. It is said that when women feel loved, they are more open to sexuality; and when men feel sexual, they open up more to love. Yes, there is some truth in this, but this is also just a stereotype. Many, many women love sex too, just as much as men. And yet there is that element of the emotional closeness, the communication, the connection with their partner that is a central part of what a woman emphasizes, what a woman likes, and what she brings into the relationship and invites her man to share with her.

B: Well, maybe you can help me with this: I had two experiences, two identical experiences in two relationships that were ten years apart. Both of these women liked to be tied to the bed with scarves. [Laughter] And it didn't excite me at all, but they just loved it.

D: Well, thank you for sharing. [Laughter]

B: So what do you do if what really gets them excited doesn't excite you at all? I'm not saying there aren't men who aren't aroused by tying up women in a sexy way. [Laughter] I mean, she wasn't handcuffed to the bed, she was just tied with beautiful silk scarves that she hand-picked herself. It was very hard for me, it was like making somebody their favorite food, and I'm allergic to it. I just felt very awkward, you know. But they were just so excited and having such a good time, I just kind of went with that.

D: Good for you, that you were able to overcome your....

B: Inhibition.

D: [Laughter] Yes, inhibitions or repressions that were there for you; or actually, in your situation, the aversion, what you didn't like. What you're bringing up is a very common issue between people; it comes up so often with the issue of desire. How much I want sex versus how much my partner wants sex. So there's always this issue of our differences and how do we work it out? I always look to a win-win arrangement—how can we both win? Now for you, I just have to hand it to you, Bill, you did a wonderful job just going along with it and simply giving them what they wanted. You gave a hundred percent to your partners by your openness to their experience, to their desire. Still, there may be times when I will not go there, when I will draw a line because it is against my values or it doesn't feel good to me. For instance, oral sex—although the majority of men and women have oral sex, less than half really find it extremely appealing.

B: Interesting.

D: Yes, it is.

B: I guess I'm not in that group, since I like oral sex. [Laughter]

D: Oh, I see.

B: I thought everybody did, you know. [Laughter]

D: So, for one partner to request oral sex is one thing—but to demand it as a requirement for feeling loved is not acceptable. No one should have to do anything that they cannot tolerate doing. That's a no-no in the area of sexuality, to do something that hurts or that's against our values. I talk to so many people about this issue of differences in desire. Often, a woman in this situation would just say, "Okay, I will give him what he wants in order to shut him up." Have you ever heard that?

B: Oh yes, yes I have. That's an old platitude, I guess. It sounds like what you're really saying is, "If you're not interested in something, you have the right to say 'no'. You don't have to do it." But, in my mind I'm thinking, "Well, but maybe I could acquire a taste for it." In other words, if I'm sensitive to what they want and see how much pleasure it gives them, as long as it doesn't hurt me. I mean, I wasn't being tied to the bed. They weren't saying, "You, Bill, have to be tied so that I can get excited." It was them who wanted to be tied. [Laughter]

D: Exactly, you were getting off pretty easy. [Laughter] So, good for you, that you were able to go along with that. On the other hand, if someone doesn't feel comfortable with something, then that needs to be okay. There are so many other ways of pleasuring each other. I really think it's a power issue when a partner says, "Oh, if you don't do this, I can't have pleasure." The truth is that sexuality is a smorgasbord of activities and excitements that are pleasureful; it's the whole experience of connection that's important. So, yes, we want to give our partner what they desire—the way you so beautifully did, Bill—and if we can't meet a specific request, then be truthful about that, be truthful in a loving way and say, "Hey, babe, I'm not willing to do this. Please know that I love you and want to please you. So, can we find other things to do that are pleasureful for you?"

I think it's so important that we don't do what's painful or unpleasant. That's such a seed for resentment. When I give in, when I do something I really don't want to—now, for you, you were really wanting to, because you wanted to please your partner—but, if I give in, my partner will know it, because I'm going to be resentful or placating. I'm not going to be into my experience in the present moment; I'm not going to be present with my partner. I've talked to many, many men who really don't want their partner to give in and do something they really don't want to. Is that how you would feel, Bill?

B: Absolutely. I'm reminded of that wonderful scene with Meg Ryan and Billy Crystal, where she says, "Yeah, I faked most of those orgasms." And that's really painful.

D: Yes, that whole thing of faking orgasms, I hope we are giving people more and more permission these days to be real. You know, 50% of women do not have orgasm through intercourse and 10% of women don't have orgasm at all. They get to that high place of extreme pleasure, but don't have a peak and then a release that is experienced as a deep relaxation. They'll just plateau at a high level and stay there. They may never ask for more than that, and some may pretend that they experience that.

The message here is to really trust our own unique way of experiencing pleasure. And if there's not pleasure, report that and allow that. Much of our national population have experienced some kind of sexual abuse or trauma: 1 of 3 of women and about 1 in 4 of men have been sexually abused. Sexual trauma, even if experienced early in life, can have a detrimental effect on a person's ability to be trusting, open, and willing to receive sexual pleasure later in life. Sexual trauma leads to a holding in, holding back, repressing our feelings, and suppressing pain. When anyone is with a partner, male or female, who has experienced some kind of sexual wounding, it's really important that the partner treat this person with a great deal of respect, tenderness, love, and consideration. There may be some vulnerabilities that arise in their sex life. If so, each person must accept and learn to work lovingly with the vulnerability, the wounding, the very deep fears that will arise when they connect on a sexual level.

One of the biggest blessings of practicing the 4 T's I shared earlier, is that by having open, honest conversations —about what's working or what's not working, as well as our personal needs and desires—gives permission for each person to be who they are. And from this place of openness and permission, healing happens, wholeness happens, people can feel affirmed for being who they are. They don't have to be perfect or make love in a certain way. We all are who we are, and we're enough just as we are.

B: Your words are very inspiring, Diana. Well, we promised to talk a little bit about lovemaking after the age of 45—so called 'middle age.' Since you and I are both over 45, I guess we're qualified to discuss it. [Laughter] A couple of days ago, several women friends of mine said to me, "Well, I've gone through menopause, my juices are dried up. Good sex is really going to be a memory. It's something that I can reflect on in the past, but it's not something I can look forward to in the future." I mentioned this to you, and you had quite a bit to say about that at the time.

D: Oh, yes! I get pretty angry when I hear that people think of people over 50 as over the hill, old maids, dirty old men.... There are still those myths and stereotypes in our culture, that sex is only for the young. In an old study by Masters and Johnson, a man who was 90 years of age fully participated in arousal, erection, and ejaculation through intercourse. He had a wonderful time with that participation. He is one of many who we would consider too old to have sex who were capable of full sexual activity. And moreover, they enjoyed the experience as much as a younger person would.

So basically, people love sex after 50, after 60, 70, 80. The body slows down, so men may take longer to get erections and have ejaculations and orgasm; women will take longer to come to orgasm. But the other side of it is, slower is pleasurable and juicy and wonder-filled. People can take time to really enjoy each other. And with the confidence and maturity they have, they can feel the time together as a truly precious gift.

B: Also implicit in this is that the experience is deeper, because it's built up over a slower period of time. I mean, I know that during a slow lovemaking, when my partner and I are very connected with each other and aware of our experience together, it's as though energy is being gathered from every part of my body—from the bottom of my feet to the top of my head. I'm collecting everything and kind of throwing it into the fire of the passion. An analogy is that I'm building a fire in a forest, and I get a log from this part of the forest and a log from that part of the forest and another log from over there, and it's all burning at the same time... it's one, big fire.

D: Yes, what you're talking about is being fully sensual; being fully in my senses on all levels. I actually do an exercise with people to help them hold their experience of the visual, the auditory, the sense of taste and smell and touch. Your poetic words speak so wonderfully of being in the moment and having our whole body be a receptor for love and a vehicle for loving. So, we must really do away with that myth—that sex is not for the aging—and realize that sex can be wonderful as people age.

Now sometimes people do lose their capacity to be sexual because of illness or disability or pain of one kind or another. I have a beautiful story about a couple who experienced this. The woman was paralyzed, and at the same time she did have the use of her fingers and her hands. Her husband would touch and suck her finger. She would have such pleasure, such arousal simply through his touch and his love. This really is a testimonial that loving and sexuality are much more a matter of the soul and the mind than the body.

B: So this supports the notion I heard—again, when I was in college—that the most powerful sex organ is the mind.

D: Oh, yes. But I would reach deeper and say the soul, the soul is the most powerful sex organ.

B: Well, now that rings true for me in my experience. I love your wisdom, Diana, and have really enjoyed our time together today. We'll have many more conversations to come, I hope, on this endlessly fascinating topic of sacred sexuality.

D: Yes, of course! And thank you, Bill. It's been wonderful to talk and laugh with you.

Chapter 6:

Playful Pathways to Sacred Sexuality

Diana speaks with Gaia Reblitz about tantra for elders, bringing playfulness to our sexuality and aging gracefully with an open heart and body.

Diana: I am so excited to talk with you today, Gaia. You are quite a role model for me about sexuality and aging. I originally met you through the tantric programs that we participated in with Steve and Lokita Carter. I would really love it if you would talk to us today about sexuality, attraction, and aging. One of the items I saw on your card is that you offer "Tantric Guidance for Elders." How did you come up with that particular niche or specialty?

Gaia: Well, first of all, it truly is my specialty since I'm a

65-year-old woman and have come to tantra at a late stage in my life—when I was 60 or 62. I studied with Steve and Lokita Carter, and then I worked with Margot Anand. What tantra brought back to me was a wonderful new opening in my life and a new found freedom. Coming back in touch with my sexuality in a spiritual and sacred way has been the greatest gift in my life in these last couple of years. Now I want to share the excitement of this path that can open up our bodies and hearts so beautifully to life. And I wanted to share it particularly with those who are older, since there are so many people at this point in time who are going through the change of life—men and women both. A lot of guidance is needed to navigate these changes. Some people can probably make it very well on their own, but I myself would have loved some guidance when I was going through menopause. [Laughter] And so, I want to share the joy of life that can come when we stay open and connected to our own sexuality, even as we age.

D: Well, I'm so excited that you're my friend and that you're willing to share your personal experience and your professional training in regard to elders, because so often, even now in this day and age, I hear people all the time saying, "I'm too old for sex." Even in the age of Viagra and all of that, people will say they're over the hill, that sex isn't a part of their life anymore. I'm curious how you came up with the title of "Tantric Guidance for Elders"?

G: I, of course, brought 'tantra' into the title because tantra is a whole pathway, a way of life, that can be shared from young age to old age, and is applicable especially for the elder generations. 'Elder' is, to me, an honoring title for people who have passed through the change of life. It's interesting that in the native tradition, in many tribes, you don't 'grow up' until you are in your 50's. Age 51 or 52 is usually the time when you are recognized as being truly adult; you become an elder. And so, I wanted to honor the age with the word 'elder'. My subtitle is "Playful Pathways to Sacred Sexuality".

D: Oh, do I love that word, 'playful' in there. So, you believe that sexuality has to do with play?

G: Yes.

D: Oh, tell me.

G: Lots and lots. [Laughter] Sexuality is our birthright. The lighter and more playful we are in accepting that natural energy of our bodies, of our hearts and minds and spirit, the deeper we can live our life. And so, I work to help people in this way of playfulness, to rediscover who they truly are.

D: I love that, Gaia. I'm thinking about my own experience as a sex therapist, and maybe you can broaden this perspective, because what I do a lot of times with people is tell them to treat each other's bodies as their plaything—as their sexual toy, if you want to use that word. In that way, people get away from the limited view of sex as 'getting off', or 'getting it on', or going for an orgasm, or trying to get pregnant. But if I can say to a person, "Use his penis as your toy, as your plaything," that can help people lighten up and really come from that place of enjoyment, juiciness, spontaneity, creativity and fun. Is that what you're meaning, Gaia?

G: Yes. And I would like to take that a little deeper and bring the sacredness into that. Our bodies are a sacred temple, a sacred tool, a sacred expression of who we truly are. And when we remember that we are the embodiment of our divine soul, of our divine identity, of the God / Goddess— however we choose to call that—then, when we meet with each other, we can come from a deep, deep appreciation, a deep, deep reverence, and an honoring place. So then the love that we share with each other becomes so deep, it can filter out all the small stuff—the little emotional reactivities that we usually get hung up in and that cause us to lose our deep, divine connection with each other. I would like to bring that connection back, the playfulness and simpleness and reverence. Tantra is a wonderful practice to help get us back to the essence of being loving with each other.

D: I hear, in your voice, your truth. I feel the depth and the honoring and the commitment you have to this path, Gaia. It's so obvious to me that you really treasure the experience of aging as a gift. So many of us in our 50's and 60's, especially women I would say, are so focused on the physical as a source of how we're valued, that we lose sight of the real preciousness of the maturing process. Would you tell us about your own personal story of what you've gained with tantra. I remember you've said that you found tantra at a time when you say that you had lost a sense of your sexuality, and your juiciness, is that right?

G: Well, I went through 10 years of total celibacy, where I didn't have any sexual connection. I tried to put it aside and went into a very deep spiritual path with Native American ceremonies. And that was good, I had deep friendships, I had a circle and family in that way. But I realized that something was deeply missing, and when I came here to Harbin Hot Springs and took my first workshop with Steve and Lokita, "Timeless Loving," I realized how much I had put a deep part of me aside. And so, in bringing that back in my life and rejoicing in being sexual, yes, and being juicy, was a wonderful discovery for me. And I discovered that being sexual and juicy has nothing to do with age.

D: You say sexuality and juiciness, from your perspective, have nothing to do with age. So, as I get wrinkles, as men lose their hair, as we get aches and pains as we get older, we're no less sexual or juicy?

G: That's right. And we are no less beautiful. For me, what happens is that we cultivate our inner beauty. It just shines out of us. The more you are in touch with yourself, the more you live from the depth of your being, which is the root chakra. That's our energy, it's a spiritual energy as well as your sexual energy. It's the ecstasy source. And the more we stay in connection with that and open it up to its fullest, the more it shines out. And wrinkles don't get in the way; wrinkles are beautiful. [Laughter] They are the signs of the painting of our life.

D: Oh, that's so poetic. I love hearing about your values, actually. They're very helpful for the ordinary person who's dealing with aging and sexuality, because it's true that sexual responses, as we age, diminish—men take longer to have erections and ejaculation, and for women, vaginal walls dry out and there can be some shrinking in the vagina, and it takes women longer to lubricate and orgasm. What do you say to people about how to find those values that you believe so strongly in? And what would you say to people about how maintain a positive outlook on aging and seeing sexuality as the total beauty of who we are?

G: The first thing I want to say is that the slower sexual response times that occur when we age can be a real positive aspect of our lovemaking with each other, because it allows us to take more time to truly play with each other, to feel each other's arousal and ecstatic fluids. It becomes a whole process that we can savor. Like you said, at one point I thought I had dried up, and, "Oh, maybe that was the end of it." But coming into partnership, I am amazed how fluid I am again.

D: Oh, that's wonderful! [Laughter]

G: It has been so easy for me to feel totally ecstatic, open, receptive, enjoying, and feeling. In a way, sexuality and orgasmic states have become incredibly deepened for me in these last years, in comparison to how I made love in my 20's, 30's, and even 40's. I find incredible new heights that I didn't know existed.

D: Mmm.

G: It takes time, yes. It involves finding another way of being with each other, a more timeless way. I have discovered that truly timeless loving, can bring us to a very open and present state. And that nurtures in a way that, again, I have not known before.

D: Isn't it true that, as a person gets older, they become more relaxed and that relaxation can contribute to a deeper and more satisfying sexual experience?

G: Right, right. That's what I've found. In my own experience, I feel so much freer nowadays than I was before. This has happened for me after turning 50 and 55. I didn't have to please anybody anymore.

D: Ahh.

G: I didn't have to live according to anybody's expectations. In some ways, I was over the hill, but it was also like starting a new life. And that kind of relaxedness and feeling at home with myself, being in acceptance with who I am, allows me to fully enjoy life and to be very present in the moment. That's a treasure.

D: I'm interested in any suggestions you have about how to develop this spiritual path, in a way that really incorporates who we are, not just what we do. Do you have any suggestions about practices, or a belief system, or a particular perspective that people can develop? For example, if people really want to start this path, how do you advise they begin?

G: Well, one of my first suggestions would be that they take a tantric workshop, whether you're single or with a partner. Any of the tantric workshops offered at Harbin Hot Springs I would always recommend. Any of Margot's workshops are incredible, and Steve and Lokita Carter are wonderful teachers. Tantric workshops are always an opening experience, and you will receive very good guidance that may be needed to help you step out of old habits that have held you back.

Another suggestion is to begin a practice of any form of meditation. This will help give you a little 'stepping back' from our tendency to get so caught up in the stress of daily life. And yoga is very helpful, especially when our bodies begin to get older. I would also suggest good food. Treat yourself well, and treat yourself to good food, not only for your body, but also for your mind and for your spirit, so that you're strong from the inside.

D: Gaia, something that I've heard more than once is that tantra is just a way to get a sexual high, that it doesn't have anything to do with spirituality. What are your thoughts about that?

G: Well, that's not how I have experienced tantra, and that's not how I teach it. Margot Anand's approach to tantra is profoundly spiritual. She trained with a spiritual master, and she really embodies, represents, and brings forth these teachings in tantra. She does that in a very spiritual context. In fact, for Margot, tantra is never just about sex. Yes, sexuality is a large part of Margot's teaching, and it's honored and remembered as being as sacred as anything in life.

D: The way that I've experienced it, Gaia, is that the tantra path is about energy.

G: Yes.

D: It's about strengthening our sexual energy and then using that energy to empower and enliven our spiritual centers. As we use that energy and uplift that energy to the 6th and 7th energy centers of our body—the spiritual energy centers—we then integrate our sexual energy for our total lives. We can use this energy for, like you say, meditation and loving ourselves and others in a deep and expanded way. Is that your point of view?

G: Yes. We also can use this energy in our creative ways of being in the world, so that we are more fully alive. And there is a cycle of aliveness that we create: we bring the sexual energy up to our crown chakra, to our spiritual energy centers, and then we bring this energy down again into our lower chakras. It's a never-ending cycle that's renewing, so we never get depleted.

D: You have a wonderful story about your painting and how your sexual energy has led you to more and more creativity. As you've heightened your sexual energy, you also have become more alive creatively. Is that right?

G: Yes, every day. My artwork is very connected to the tantra path, because I am painting mandalas that bring out the ancient tantric symbols, called yantras, which are energy patterns of divine creation and divine manifestation. Painting for me is such a joy and a fulfillment, and I feel also very humble, very privileged, that I'm allowed to bring these yantras out into the world in the best form of beauty, balance, and radiance that I can.

D: How wonderful. What a gift you have, Gaia, a real blessing. In the time we have left, I'd like to touch a little bit upon an aspect of men's aging process. I'm talking about a success orientation and value for performance that leads men a lot of times to performance anxiety, especially as they lose some of their vigor of earlier years. There are some men who accept that they don't have that big erection any longer, and they and their partner find enjoyment in his entering her soft. And then there are men who resist and go for one of the miracle drugs, like Viagra, that's going to give them the big hard on of a young man. My question is, from your standpoint, what would you say to men about this?

G: Well, my first approach would be look at high sex, which doesn't emphasize the performance, but rather the connection. I would say to the performance-oriented men to re-orient from performance to pleasuring, to celebrating, playing, and even praying with each other as you join your bodies. There is so much unexplored wonder, enjoyment, and fulfillment in that, that the performance part—which is so much in the mind, you know—can never bring to you. I think there's a huge exploration of sexuality as we age that men can engage in. Aging actually helps both men and women to change their relationship to sexuality and to deepen it. What is really helpful is to come from that place of God and Goddess within us. We can play that out in our sexual encounters.

D: So, Gaia, are you saying that orgasm and ejaculation aren't the goals of tantric sexuality?

G: I would say that the experience of orgasm can expand so much when we get away from what we used to call the Big 'O', the big orgasm. There are so many rich, subtle kinds of orgasm, and we often miss out on them because we're so focused on the big climax and release.

D: Oh, that's well said. Thank you, Gaia, you have given us such heart-centered gifts today, and I certainly appreciate all you've shared—your expertise, your wisdom, your experience, and particularly yourself. Thank you so much for blessing us with your presence today.

G: Thank you, too, Diana. And much love to you.

Chapter 7:

Tantra & Transformation
in Everyday Life

A conversation with Suzie Heumann, creator of Tantra.com, about the rich wisdom of the Kama Sutra and how tantra education can transform the quality of our daily lives.

Diana: I am delighted and honored to be talking today with Suzie Heumann, who is a wonderful author and radio commentator, and actually has done so much for tantra education for the ordinary person through her wonderful books called The Everything Great Sex Book and The Everything Kama Sutra Book. She has done numerous radio interviews, and is a syndicated writer and award-winning video producer. I think her greatest contribution, however, is the website Tantra.com, which just celebrated its ten-year anniversary. It reaches thousands of people world-wide, with the commitment to serve everyone seeking to grow and transform their consciousness through sacred sexual practices and conscious intimacy. In Suzie's words, she and Tantra.com want more love in the world. So, I feel blessed, Suzie, that you're with us today. Thank you so much for joining us.

Suzie: Well, thank you for that glowing introduction, Diana. I really appreciate it. This has all been a long, wonderful adventure that seems to have a long way to go.

D: I was telling you earlier that I actually see you as the mother of sacred sexuality, Suzie—someone who birthed an idea and a vision ten years ago, when it wasn't really popular to do that; to talk about the blend of sexuality, spirituality, love, and intimacy. You've taken the whole realm of sacred sexuality from a baby, nurtured and developed it, and now you have a wonderful vision and vehicle for spreading information about sacred sexuality throughout the world. Would you talk a bit about your initial vision for Tantra.com and what your vision is for your organization today?

S: Well, being a mother of three beautiful young women, maybe it was just natural that I took on something as difficult as educating people about sacred sexuality, love and intimacy, tantra, and the Kama Sutra through the highly technical vehicle of the internet.

In the world today, there is an astounding amount of pornography, and it has actually fueled the technology in the world of the internet; and yet it's just viewed as pornography. We have women's magazines that are selling all kinds of sex ideas and clichéd kinds of practices and tips. But the real world of sexuality education hasn't really existed until more recently, especially the notion of sacred sexuality.

So, in the last ten years, I think we've seen a huge increase in that. But, in a way, the sacred aspect of sexuality has been slow on the uptake. And when we first started the site ten years ago—and I thank my husband Michael for having the foresight to sense what the web would be, because in 1995, very few people even knew what the world wide web was.

So, we registered the URL Tantra.com, and a few years later Tantra.org. Well, Michael quickly went off and started doing other things, but I took over the building and the running of this business. My vision for it was getting the idea of sacred sexuality out there. In the early years, when we first started the business, we had a few books and videos, mostly from the tantra teachers that were known at the time, like Margot Anand. Most importantly, we connected people through simple, personal programs, discussion boards, and various ways to contact people. We offered a whole lot of free learning.

D: And what were you hoping might grow out of the web site?

S: Well, in the first couple of years I was hoping to unite the tantra community and have a venue where people could connect with each other and teachers of tantra. So my hope for it was to be a venue of connection.

A couple of years after we started the business online, and as the internet grew, magazines started coming to me: Cosmopolitan and some other large magazines. And they started asking for interviews, because the notion of sacred sexuality was new to them. But the policy in those large magazines was never to give out much information about who they were interviewing. So they never gave out our web address or email address. For years, I was doing these big, high-profile interviews, and maybe the word tantra or Kama

Sutra would get out there, but not the website address. From this experience, I felt I had to give it up, to give up the notion that I was going to let the world know about tantra on a grand scale. I had to sit back and hope that they would find the website. But also, I knew my interviews were pure education to those they reached.

As the years have gone by, traffic to the website has grown. It has educated the world about words like the Kama Sutra, tantra, sacred sexuality, and all the more esoteric words as well. In ten years it's changed, quite powerfully. The philosophy has changed. But one of the things that we always wanted to do, that was my vision, was to move into online learning. We wanted to do that in 1999. Now, heaven forbid, about 2% of the population was on high speed internet at that time. So it probably wouldn't have worked then. When the dot-com crash happened in the middle of 2001, we just kind of had to go along with things. Then, two years ago, I realized that broadband and high speed internet was getting out there. More and more people had it. That's when we started building an online learning area, which was our original vision.

And that's what we've been really involved in for the last year and a half; building a learning environment—it's not nearly complete, never will be, but, boy, it's the thing that we are really aiming for and focusing on. It's a wonderful vehicle, because a lot of people around the world are now hooked up to broadband, but they don't have the money and the resources by which to send expensive DVDs to their country overseas: Asia, India, places like that. And so we're noticing that a lot of people who are in our online membership area and our learning area (that streams educational audio and video), are coming from around the world, literally. That makes me feel really good. The word tantra itself means 'to weave'. What a wonderful metaphor for tantra education on the web, the world-wide web, the web of integration and expansion. So, it's all coming back around to the central vision. And I'm loving it. It really fuels me.

D: I can tell you love it through your voice, Suzie. Your enthusiasm is contagious. I'm curious about how you do this dance of communicating about sexuality. How do you keep that vision alive, in light of the way our Western society tends to separate spirituality from sexuality? There's the idea that sexuality is bad and dirty and wrong, there are all these values that separate sexuality and spirituality. Spirituality is in the church, it's what you do when you go to church on Sundays. Given all of this, I really admire your willingness to step out there, Suzie, in the masses where you could be misunderstood by those who tend to see any kind of sexuality on the web as pornographic. How do you walk that fine line? How do you do that dance?

S: Well, I might have been in serendipity. But I would say that it's been a learning process for me, especially during the first four or five years that the business was growing, when we were expanding, and I was doing those magazine interviews. I learned in the process how to handle the media. I think what helped most, Diana, is the background that I had already—many, many years of studying with Western Tantric teachers, working with them, working deeply with them, within a community that we were involved with. If I hadn't done such deep Tantric work in the past, I don't know that I would have been able to hold that clear of a vision. And so I honor all that teaching and work that got me to this place, and I try to transmute it through me and the people that work with me.

The site has remained a portal where people can come to find out information about sacred sexuality. And if I hadn't had all the background, if I hadn't known this deepest part in myself, if I hadn't had all these transformational experiences with some of the simplest practices, I wouldn't have this strength of commitment behind me. I know that this stuff works, and it's so simple! Sometimes it's just a simple turn of a key for a person. Some key that can boost them to looking deeply into their life and life experiences, and give them a transformational gateway into something they might never have experienced in their life. That can be the simplest of practices.

D: What are one or two of the key learnings that you've received over the years from your teachers, experiences you've had with sacred sexuality that can transform consciousness through sexuality?

S: Well, I think the key for me is a deep understanding of the chakra system, not only its esoteric, but its physical manifestations. Just feeling them in your body, even sitting up straight and imagining your chakras all lined up. You can even look at a chart of them, you know, in front of you. Just sitting and feeling them. Another really great practice is basic, simple, conscious breathing. Once you know them intimately, you can check in with yourself ten, twenty times a day. "How am I breathing? Where is my breath? Is my mind following my breath?" Those simple little check-ins with the breath lead to a profoundly deeper kind of witnessing of oneself. And that, I think, can be a really meaningful yet simple daily practice for the third of us who are Cultural Creatives, who want to know more about life, who want to know more about ourselves and are willing to push some of our boundaries to discover our shadow sides, our light sides—all the mix of who we are as an individual. When we have practices that are simple throughout our day, that cause us to witness ourselves not in a judging way, but just,

"Oh, there I am," the more we get into states of being where we want to be during the day.

D: Yes, isn't that true?

S: Yes, at each given moment. Also, I think that the Tantric practice of truly opening up your eyes and seeing the other as oneself is transformative. It is the hardest thing we can ever do, Diana, to look at a person, to really see them, and to open ourselves to them. I would say too that learning as much as we can about our own bodies opens us to the experience of sacred sexuality. We begin to understand that it is we who are responsible for all of our pleasures in our lives: our sexual pleasure, our social pleasure, our enjoyment of life. My pleasure is only my responsibility. My successes, my virtue, my happiness are all my responsibility, not someone else's. Not the church's, not my partner's, not my parents', not my boss'; they're my responsibility.

I think one of the more freeing experiences that can transport you to the dissolving realms is literally learning to open up your voice. Open up your fifth chakra and allow your body to say what it means. I don't necessarily mean that it's good to do this in all kinds of communication. But when it comes to love-making, really, really opening up and breaking open that barrier that keeps us in sort of a meek, mild expression of our pleasure. We're so often stuck in our throat. When we are expressing with a high-pitched breathing voice, we can get stuck in our higher chakras, with little or no connection to the lower chakras, which ground us in our experience. But when we open up our voice, we allow the sexual energy to flow in all the pleasure realms, the higher as well as the lower. Then you feel your whole body vibrating, and that's the place that has you opening up your higher chakras, but definitely opening up your lower chakras as well.

The energy spectrum of the seven chakras is what Margot Anand calls the Inner Flute. In sacred sexuality, we learn to open up, let our energy expand, and let it flow throughout the body. This is a transformational experience that will literally send you into a place of freedom—a freedom of expression, body, mind, soul. It's just the freedom that's recognized. I think that's part of what the Tantric experience is. It's about understanding that you're absolutely part of the web. Everything is one. And I can produce a freedom and a joy for myself that then transforms the rest of my life.

D: And that we don't have to be afraid of being hurt, being laughed at, or being disapproved of. I know that from my work with my clients as a sex therapist, one of the things I see a lot is fear. I think that when we open up these ecstatic places in ourselves, it's not just the bliss that we encounter; it's also the shadow, the fears, the pain, the past repression that we have. These practices, as well as the awareness that you're talking about, can help us to open up to all of who we are and to all of who our Beloved is.

I've done a practice of moving to really basic, earthy drum music with a former lover. We stood back-to-back, and we were just pulsing—moving our knees up and down, breathing, and being in sync with our breath and our movements. We had had a lovers' quarrel the night before; I had felt very rejected by him and had not wanted to have anything to do with him sexually or emotionally, I was so deeply feeling my fear. Through this practice of breathing and feeling the first chakra of preservation, sexuality and survival, and the second chakra of strength, emotion, and connection to another, I took that energy to my power center in my third chakra. I connected to my own ability to be responsible and to take care of myself. I lost my fear, and I also started harmonizing with his energy. I felt the blending and the connecting, and was able, then, to see him more clearly as someone who really wanted the best for me, who loved me in the way he could love me. Most of all, I got in touch with how I loved myself, and how I wanted to be loving to him (my fourth chakra, the heart center). I found too that through that process, I really got in touch with my own values. This was not verbal, we didn't talk about it, we just did this breath practice and my fear was transformed.

S: And you got in sync through the breath practice. That's exactly why drumming is one of the oldest forms of Shamanic transformation. It fills our body cavity with a resonance that causes us to start vibrating in the same frequency—everything that's in fear of that drumming, of that beat, gets onto the same vibration. That's the Shamanic world, literally. I think that's one of the reasons why there were secret rites in tantra in ancient times. You had to pass a lot of tests and go through a lot of work before you were deemed responsible enough to enter the sexual mysteries.

D: Suzie, I know that you have a commitment to both tantra in general, and the Kama Sutra of India in particular. Would you please talk about what the Kama Sutras, and then how it is actually a part of the bigger picture of how to live life?

S: Yes. I wanted to address one more thing, but it's kind of a good segue actually. I think we Westerners are really hurt in our second chakras. We're really hurt around sexuality. We each have to reinvent the wheel for ourselves. No one teaches us about sexuality, and, consequently, the average person doesn't get very far in their sexual education in life before they put it aside and sublimate it for other things. So, really, when we're teaching Western tantra, we're starting with sexuality because that's the hook for people. It was taught in ancient tantra that our sexual nature is the hardest place to end duality. But sexuality is a metaphor for the rest of life. Anything we're doing in tantra in the sexual realm is a direct metaphor for how we're working in the rest of our lives.

Very often, in Western Tantric teachings, you go to workshops, you work with the teacher, you're following some of the teachings—you're going straight for the sexuality level first. As you progress, you get that it's a metaphor. You get that it's life enhancing in all of the arenas of your life, because you're learning better communication, you're learning better what you need in life, you're learning better how to see the other as divine. It just expands and expands and expands. So, tantra is a metaphor. And I think beyond sex education, tantra is one of the bigger important functions for my understanding, of myself. The Kama Sutra was one part of four parts of knowledge that the higher castes in ancient Indian and Hindu culture studied. The Kama Sutra means, 'short aphorisms' or 'sayings'. 'Kama' means pleasure, and particularly pleasure in sexuality. Kama was enjoyment of all the forms of pleasure—visiting with friends, having parties, playing games, your sensual pleasure, all the things that bring you pleasure, of which sex is one. The Kama Sutra delineates how you court a woman, how you court a man, how you treat your wife, how you treat your husband—all of that, in addition to aphrodisiacs, the positions, and the acts of love.

We think of Kama Sutra as position. That's only one small part of the whole Sutras. Along with the Kama Sutra came the Artha. 'Artha' means 'your means to wealth'—success, the family, the acquisition of material goods, and self-realization on a social or active level. So often in the tantra community, I found that people felt marginalized around making money and bringing money to themselves. I think it's been one of the holes, one of the places that have not been addressed enough in Western tantra. I used to see these big holes for people, but really, in a holistic-like life, which we all are striving for, having work that fills you—that fulfills you in life—but also brings you money, was an important thing in Hindu life. If you didn't have enough money to support a family, to support your pleasure in life, and to support you on a material plain, you didn't have enough free time to do the third part of the Sutras, which was the Dharma Sutra: dharma work, the duty work, the virtue you bring to your life, your helping of your village and community, your moral level, your honesty, your tolerance, and your charity to others less wealthy than you. If you didn't have money, you didn't have time to go out into your community and help your community, so you had to have enough money to have pleasure and to do your duty in life.

Those three things work together to bring a balanced life to the human being. And the fourth part of this was moksha, which is the final, total liberation from the chains of existence—the chains of rebirth and death, and rebirth and death. The better you lived your kama, artha, and dharma, the more you did away with your rebirth cycle, and you got further toward your total liberation. So, those three things work together, and I think that we often have an unbalanced wheel, so to speak. In coaching, they use a wheel that I think is divided into eight pieces, and each is an aspect of your life. (See the Wheel of Life diagram on page 206.) You rate them on a scale from one to ten—one being the closest in the center of the circle, and 10 being the outermost. If you've got family life that's taking up a six or a seven, but your sexuality life is down at a two or a three, you begin to quickly see where you need to heal and balance more. I'd like to offer people the idea of using a wheel for these three parts of their life, dividing a circle into three parts—dharma, artha, and kama with moksha in the middle to signify what we're aiming for. Then look at your life from that standpoint. Analyze it a little bit and ask, "Where am I out of balance? And where might I fulfill my dharma wheel and make it more even, so that I feel accomplished and full at the end of my life, not just in the pleasure area alone?"

D: That's really interesting, Suzie. As I hear you talk, it seems to me that in India, there was a focus on the balance and the integration of all three of the Sutras to get to the fourth level—the moksha. I believe that the Western culture, and the United States in particular, isolates and separates pleasure. We make it something that we can only do if our work is done, that we have to earn the right to have pleasure by working hard enough. I think we're still conflicted in our society about pleasure.

S: Yes, very much so.

D: It's relegated to something that's private and so personal. I was thinking, as you were talking earlier about the Kama Sutra and sacred sexuality, that people don't want to admit that they don't know everything about sexuality. They will endure years of ignorance and lack of information, or endure a lot of pain for a long, long time because they don't want to admit that they don't know enough in the area of sexuality. It seems that India really admitted that we are pleasure-oriented beings, that they really had the perspective of pleasure being sacred. Is that right?

S: Yes. And as Nick Douglas said so aptly in Sexual Secrets, we have a temple. We are given a fantastic body. It doesn't have billions of nerve endings for no reason. So, to then treat it as a temple, and move from that avenue of honoring it, that it might have some gateways for us to higher knowledge, is a silly thing to deny. I think in this culture, we have definitely done that, through our religious and cultural background. We're a melting pot in the United States, we have many different cultural backgrounds coming together, and that can be confusing to people, even to a couple. We don't have a long-standing ideology around these things, like the ancient Indians did and even to a degree in modern days. And so, again, that's often why we call sacred sexuality a healing dichotomy, because we're healing a lot of misunderstanding there. We're healing the physical body, emotional hurt, shame, and all the confusing multiples and multiples of layers that our melting pot has put on us.

I think that's breaking down now, to some degree. And I find that on an individual level, I can't tell you how many times I've heard from people who say, "I tried a simple practice, and I cannot believe how simple it was to get in touch again with the full spectrum of feelings inside of me." And how many people have said, "I read a couple of articles on the website. I had no idea what this was, but, I tell you, I always knew there was something much more important about sex." I am seeing today that people in our culture are generally much more transformational, much more grounded in depth. We're having more transcendental experiences. I have read in some current polls that about 33-34% of the population, all ages, report having had some sort of out-of-body experience during sex.

D: Really?

S: Some kind of transformational moment. That's why the ancient tantrics knew that sexuality was a potent place to develop, and expand, and to continue to expand.

D: So, if sexuality is a portal to our expanded consciousness, how do the other Sutras fit in? Is it that the sexual experience comes first in the Indian culture? Or does wealth—building wealth—come first? How does it all fit together?

S: You are asking a question that has been argued in the classic Hindu books. They would have fascinating arguments about it, and one would argue for kama. Bima, I think, Arjuna's right-hand man and soldier, would argue that kama was the most important, because without love and pleasure, you never sought to take a wife—now this is from a man's point of view—and if you never sought to take a wife, you would not have the impetus to start a business, to grow your wealth, to build a home. You would never have a family, the children, and the legacy that would inspire you to want to go do your dharma work in your community, to do your give-away work, and give back to your community. Without a family, you wouldn't see the advantage of it, because you didn't have a lineage coming back to you. So I'm personally on Bima's side. I think kama comes first. But each of the infamous people in the classic stories of creation, in Hinduism, all argued for one or the other. So it's an ongoing mystery.

D: How fascinating! Suzie, I really appreciate your articulation and definition of the issues in this debate. As I listen to you talk about it, I'm thinking about the biological impulses that certainly are connected with sexuality for reproduction, as well as the need to gather up money and food for survival. So, it seems to me that there might be some biological drive in both of these areas of development.

S: Diana, these relate to the major sections of the chakras. The lower chakras, and then the heart-centered chakras, and then the higher knowledge chakras.

D: Would you be more specific about that, Suzie? Some people aren't familiar with the chakra system, so could you delineate the different chakras and their use, and then how they relate to the Sutras.

S: Well, when you consider that artha means wealth-building, success, family, and the acquisition of material goods, that's our base chakra. That's our first chakra. We can't have sex, procreate, we can't be in our hearts, we can't be critical thinkers—any of those higher functions—unless we've got a roof over our head, some food in our stomachs, and have addressed the ongoing first chakra survival issues.

D: Yes, I see.

S: Artha and the means for wealth-building also involve our second and third chakras. Our second chakra has to do with creativity. When we get creative in the enjoyment of the work we do in the world, that brings us not only money but it brings us self-fulfillment, hopefully. And the third chakra, which is our empowerment chakra—our will—is very important in wealth-building in the artha world. In the kama world, we would look at the first and second chakras—the centers of pleasure, sexuality, and creativity. We would look at the heart chakra—the fourth chakra. And we would actually look at the fifth chakra—the self-expression chakra, because, don't forget that kama has to do with your social activities also.

When you look at dharma, you're looking at the higher chakras. You're looking at the heart chakra. You're looking at virtue and speaking virtue—the fifth chakra. Your sixth chakra is more about connecting the body with the mind, and bringing the mind to bear on virtue, morality, honesty, tolerance, and courage. So you're involving the higher chakras in the dharma. And, of course, moksha, is related to the seventh chakra, where you're really living in a space of oneness with everything already. This is how they roughly correspond.

D: How elegant, to delineate them that way. I'm pretty amazed at the unity of energy that the chakras represent and that the sutras represent. I can see that all of the chakras are included in the four sutras. It's pretty wonderful.

S: Well, the ancients had a long time to put together a very wonderful system, with Ayurvedic medicine, Jyotish astrology, and the concepts by which they felt, literally, an upstanding citizen should live by, where all the pieces are included.

D: From your experience with Tantra.com, the Indian culture, and the Kama Sutra, what would you say is missing in our society that we don't have this integration of pleasure, wealth, and service that leads to liberation? What's missing here? We really don't get it here.

S: Yes. Well, I think again, we come back to the idea of balancing these three—the dharma, artha, and kama. But we don't have such a balanced valuing of these in our Western cultures. Primarily because of the religious principles that this country and Europe were built on. The Protestant work ethic, for example, says, "Work very hard. Work, work, work, to have money. Work, work. And then maybe you'll have a little time left over for pleasure." The Christian overlay says, to its benefit, "Go out in your community and give away some of that wealth. Give away some of your time to help the needy. Work at the soup kitchen line. Help with the rummage sale at your church three times a year and donate."

So we've got artha and dharma pretty darn well covered. But, where is the balance? In the last twenty-five years, we've seen more women and mothers going to the workplace to supplement the family's income. Their time to give to pleasurable activities has vanished. The economy has gotten so tight for middle- and lower-income people. And the amount of money we can spend on pleasurable activities has diminished as a result. Now work and career can be a great thing for women—don't get me wrong. But what it often means is that somebody else—at least for a portion of the day—is raising our children.

D: Yes, so many children are being raised by people outside of their biological families.

S: Yes, so money's gotten tighter, and it has crowded out pleasure. Also, this idea of pleasure for itself, being a pure entity and something that is good for us, goes against the Christian ideal. And Christianity kind of runs the country. It's really too bad that, through the religious influence on how we live our lives, we have learned to deny the pleasure aspect of our lives. I say pleasure, I'm not talking just about sexuality and intimacy—although these are really, really important facets of a happy life—I'm talking about all forms of pleasure, of treating ourselves well.

The number one complaint for young couples and older couples is: "Where do we find the time? How do we carve the time out for a four-hour ritual love-making? "Sounds good! But how do we do it? As a culture, we don't put enough emphasis on caring for ourselves in those ways— taking the time to have a women's group once a month, having the time to get a massage, making time to take yourself on a walk with a girlfriend or a boyfriend—we don't emphasize enough the value of treating ourselves thus. We let it fly in our lives. And that makes a less than whole human being.

D: Yes, Suzie, yes. I agree with you that pleasure is necessary for our wholeness, for our well-being, for our happiness and fulfillment. And, like you say, pleasure can be so many different things. It really can be easily added to our daily activities, some little bright spot of a pleasant experience. So to explore this a bit, Suzie, how does the Kama Sutra's art of pleasure-making relate to my ordinary, everyday life?

S: Well, very simply, the breath. It is a very good place to begin. One of the things about checking in with your breath ten, twenty times a day—"How am I breathing, how am I feeling about that?"—is that when you start witnessing those moments, then you start seeing the moment-moment-moment, and you're in the moment more.

D: Yes, the energy of pleasure, sexuality, and presence is about unity. When I really get into my senses and feel the connection with a friend who I'm hugging, I feel their heart, I smell their hair, I hear their voice, and my heart is fed.

S: Yes!

D: I don't think we pay enough attention to those moments.

S: We don't! So when you give that hug, and you smell their smells, and you linger in the hug for a moment, just kind of dropping in and melting with them and dissolving—the two of you dissolving—that's something we can allow ourselves to experience fully, with no other thoughts. That's kama. That's pleasure. This society of ours is very fast moving, very anxious to get the work done, and plan the next day, and "what does my calendar say", and "where do I have to be next?" We are always out in front of ourselves or lingering in our past hurts. We're very rarely in the moment. Kama is about being in the moment.

D: Oh, very well put. And I also think kama—being in the moment—is what wholeness is. It's what spirituality is. It's what loving is. It's being right here, right now, in this moment. This is all we have, and this is enough. I find that as I let go of the past and the future—of the subject-object orientation, the difference between you and me—and really experience our unity and our connection, I am so much more right where I am, loving myself, loving others, and loving life in this moment. This is what happens when I can really see the person I'm with, whether it's my lover or my child or a friend. And this also occurs when I'm by myself and seeing myself as my own Beloved in the moment—that's what ultimate fulfillment is. These experiences help me expand, open, transcend, and be fully present in myself and this experience.

S: Yes. And I think that when pleasure and sexuality are truly sacred, you can recognize each of those moments. The smaller the perceived pleasure—the simpler the pleasure—I go after. This is a practice of mine, not to be going after the bigger pleasure, but the smaller, simpler pleasures. So I often will go outside, when it's mildly windy. I particularly love fall and winter for this. I'll go outside for a short walk on my property. I'll meditate for a few minutes, but then I'll throw my arms wide open and literally start breathing with the trees. When there's a little bit of wind, you can imagine the trees breathe. The leaves are rustling, and that's an in-breath. Then they stop, and that's an out breath. This is one of my favorite simple pleasures, to breathe with the trees.

It may sound kind of silly, but I like to put myself as one and the same with nature. I get as close as I can to feeling the intimacy of being a natural thing in a natural setting, of being an integral part of that scene. For me, that's the universal unity that I thrive in, to then be able to see any person as the same as me, to see all things in this way: rocks, computers, trees, animals. We're all essentially the same. And the less we have boundaries around that, I think the better for understanding the ultimate sacredness of all acts, including our loving, sexual nature.

D: This is what tantra teaches, and what the Kama Sutra teaches as well, is that right?

S: Tantra teaches this more of the two. The Kama Sutra is more about, "Here's this, this, and this to do." The Dharma Sutra talks about virtue and doing good in the world. But it's really the Tantric practices that are all about dissolving with the oneness.

D: It's very beautiful, Suzie. The way you have expressed this feels, to me, like a prayer. I could talk to you for hours and hours.

S: Yes, me too! I'm loving it!

D: I'm loving it, too. It seems to me that you've just prayed—and I think we've prayed together—through our conversation...

S: It feels that way, doesn't it?

D: It really does. I'm thinking again of that metaphor of you as a mother of sacred sexuality who has brought this vision of loving in a whole way—loving, connecting with the trees, the wind, yourself, and your partner—and bringing this way of being to others through education. That's an opportunity we all have, and you so beautifully live that through your life. And I'm curious, Suzie, since it's the new year, what is your New Year's wish for our society?

S: My wish is that every person has the ability, time, and potential for working towards their own self-realization. I hope that in our society, we begin to create more balance in our work world, our family world, our community world, our sexuality world, our private time world; and that all the things that we do in our lives are guided by a deeper understanding of our own self-realization—our own sense of, "Who am I, in the deepest sense? What can I bring to the world?" That's the ultimate life for all of us.

D: Beautifully said, Suzie. You're speaking about the reverence for life that each of us can cultivate by loving ourselves, each other, and all of life, and through the understanding that comes about ourselves and the world through those practices. And from the understanding comes the unity.

S: That's right! That's right. Exactly! And there we have another circle.

D: Yes, isn't that wonderful? And thank you, Suzie, for your time today. I congratulate you not only for your vision, but for the nurturing of your vision for all of us, by bringing to fullness growth experiences that we all can take advantage of so easily. So thank you.

S: You're welcome, Diana. And thank you so much for this time with you, I've enjoyed our talk.

Interview Commentary with Diana and Bill

D: Bill, I was so excited to have the opportunity to talk with Suzie Heumann. She obviously is committed to living a healthy, loving, responsible, and respectful life. She's also interested in sharing that with everyone she comes in contact with—which is what her vision and her commitment are. I received an email from Suzie about a month ago announcing the tenth anniversary of Tantra.com. In her email, she talks about the commitment of Tantra.com, which is to serve everyone who is seeking to grow and transform their consciousness through sacred sexual practices and conscious intimacy. "We want more love in the world," is what she shared. She said also that the vision of Tantra.com is to be a world-class resource for people to access and learn more about sacred sexuality, tantra, and the Kama Sutra. "At the center of this learning, the individual develops the inner core that radiates love, compassion, understanding, sensual pleasure, and personal empowerment." What I see is that Suzie really walks her talk about the experience of sexuality as sacred with all of life—with the values of love, compassion, and understanding.

B: I think what's so interesting is her vision of an online university, which of course is something that we're forming at LovingWay.net. She talked about how, in the beginning, it was difficult to create a learning environment on the internet because there wasn't that much broadband or high speed internet available. We see now, of course, with the increase in high speed internet for so many people, that now is the time to do it. So many lights in this wonderful area of tantra and human sexuality are starting to become illuminated. That's what I'm seeing.

D: Yes. I feel so grateful for the way in which Suzie is leading the way by offering education and venues of connection for people like me, who really believe in the power of tantra to transform people's lives. My personal vision, too, is to communicate that power, and to make available that opportunity for people to learn online.

My book, *Soulful Sex: Weaving Sex, Spirit and Love into Everyday Life*, describes my own personal experiences of transformation through tantra, as well as other people's. I really believe in learning through stories and through doing. So part of the process of learning through my book will be having homework exercises that help people implement activities that can deepen their understanding of what sacred sexuality is, and how to apply it in their lives for their own personal fulfillment and growth.

B: Well, I certainly look forward to those. I noticed that in the beginning of your talk, Suzie talked about some key practices. She talked about checking in with the breath several times a day. She talked about being responsible for all the pleasures in your life—sexual, social, and personal. What I particularly liked—and what I'm going to ask you to comment on—is this notion of making noise when we're feeling pleasure. We can be stuck in the throat, stuck in the higher chakras, but at the same time be closed in the lower chakras. But if we open the first three chakras also, then the pleasure experience becomes much more deep and satisfying. I found that really interesting and exhilarating.

D: I did, too, Bill, and I'm so appreciative that you asked about that, because breath, movement, sound, and presence are the four keys to a complete tantra experience of integrating our spiritual energy and our sexual energy. If we don't open up our ability to express ourselves verbally with a lot of sound—not just a little sound—we're stuck in the upper levels of our energy, which then doesn't ground it and make it full and strong. When we really open up our sound and express it fully and gutturally and deeply, we open the lower chakras and ground the sexual energy.

And people don't want to do that, because we're taught that it's impolite. In love-making—which is personal and private—I've found, in my sex therapy work, people don't make sounds. But in order to have a full-bodied orgasm, sound is important. It's connected to the breath, and it also brings the energy down—like Suzie so beautifully said—to the first and second and third chakras, the areas of survival and sexuality and power. So we start integrating all of that energy and letting it flow, letting it move, which allows us to have full sensations, and full experience.

B: Doesn't that self consciousness around making noise come from people having sexual episodes furtively; where Mom and Dad are in the bedroom, the door is locked, and they don't want the children to hear them? Or when we're growing up in our teenage years, and we're having sex in the back seat of a car? Or masturbating and not wanting people to know that we're doing that?

D: I think it does come from the attitude that our society places on sexuality: that it's for married people in the bedroom, who are between the ages of twenty-one and sixty years of age, who are healthy, strong, and intelligent.

B: That's a very specific and rather rigorous criteria.

D: It leaves out single people. If you think about it, people who are single and who are sexual are often hyped-up by the media as loose or perverted. There's this back and forth between the movie stars who are single, living with their partners, and having babies. They're idolized on the one hand as free and liberated beings, but on the other hand, there's usually a hidden disgust—or not so hidden disgust and disrespect. So single people are seen as non-sexual, as well as disabled people, the handicapped, old people, overweight people, poor people.

B: Yes, it is a kind of discrimination. I see it over and over again. We as a culture, in Western civilization, are not over it, yet.

D: Well, it's interesting, the stereotypes of women being valued in our society for their beauty, and men for their wealth.

B: Right.

D: Especially men, people who are not wealthy, are not seen as particularly as valuable in our society. So I think there's a lot of distortion of what value is, and what health is, what sexuality and pleasure are, who it's for, and how it's applied and expressed.

B: Here's a question: Suzie said that sexuality is the most difficult place to end duality. Why don't you comment on that?

D: I think she was referring to the idea that sexuality separates us when we see ourselves as separate from our experience or separate from another person. Our society defines life in terms of opposites: good and bad, right and wrong, rich and poor, happy and sad. We so naturally think in terms of opposites. The opposite of sexuality in our society is spirituality. This is an enormous duality we have not yet healed as a society. Our society tends to think of sexuality as just about the body, about having pleasure and getting off sexually. People so often define spirituality, or loving, or what is good, or what is a connecting experience, as different from being sexual.

I think also that sexuality is the most difficult area to end duality because it's one of the strongest energies there is. I think to end the duality, there needs to be an integration of just what tantra and the Kama Sutra are speaking to. Tantra recognizes that sexuality is our ability to express love through our bodies and through our lives. It recognizes that we are inherently good with our bodies. It teaches us to accept everything about ourselves and our lives as sacred. The Kama Sutra shows us how we do this in specific ways in our sexual lives as well as our daily lives.

B: I think it's interesting that the fourth sutra is moksha, the aspect of liberation. Suzie said that, according to all these sutras, liberation equals the balance between pleasure, wealth, and the ability to be philanthropic, to help in society. I like what she said about this, that you have to have enough money to do philanthropy and time for pleasure. In my opinion, you have to have enough money just to have time to do Tantric practices.

D: Yes.

B: So, I really found that meaningful. I also found interesting what she said about the poll, in which 33-34% of people who have peak sexual experiences, experience them as a profound out-of-body experience—a sort of trans-personal experience.

D: Yes. Isn't it great that she has this statistic to show that sexuality is a natural experience of not only being in the body, but transcending the body? So it's both! It's as though the ecstatic experience and the heightened energy that comes through sexuality, can also take us to heavenly realms. It's long been written about and researched, that these transcendent experiences can happen through sexuality. How wonderful that we are able to see sexuality as more than just the experience of pleasure. Not that pleasure in itself is not wonderful and good, in fact, her definition of the Kama Sutra says that pleasure is one of the three portals that lead us to liberation. At the same time, we recognize that it is a doorway also to transcendence. So there is a unity in that, that we're in the body, and not of the body, at the same time.

B: Yes, that's an excellent point. And you know, Diana, we have the sex organs and all of those nerve bundles available to us. One can have a very pedestrian experience, as you said, of just achieving sexual discharge. Or one can literally be transported to the transcendent realms. This is true of other practices. For example, we all have lungs that we use to breathe air. And people such as Stanislav Grof, Jacquelyn Small, and other rebirthers, have turned the breath into a sacred path to realization. It seems that we're given, in this life and in this body, all these tools of transformation. And I guess it's up to us to find out how many ways they can be used.

D: Right! I've come to understand tantra as a wonderful spiritual path, particularly for people who are being sexual regularly, because it helps us relate to our sexual pleasure as spiritual. It helps us to relate to our bodies and to every aspect of life as spiritual, as vehicles of the divine. As you were saying, Bill, we have the opportunity to use so many different tools for our spiritual development and our evolution. How wonderful that we have Sacred Sexuality as one tool that affirms the body and affirms all of life! It doesn't designate just positive, pleasureful experiences as divine. It invites us to see all of life, even the pain and the problems and the shadow of our lives, as gifts that are divinely made and helpful to our growth and our sacredness.

B: Well, one of your chief teachings, Diana, is that the structures in our personality—the resistances to pleasure—show up when we have great pleasure. So, if we want to be on an upward spiral evolution of a pleasure path like tantra, then of course we have to deal ongoingly with everything that stands in the way of our happiness. I think that's why the tantra path is a path of celebration. It is a path that says, "Happiness is possible in the hundred years that most people can hope to live."

Suzie said that Americans don't take time for a four-hour love making ritual any more than they take walks through nature. And, of course, for those of us in the tantra community, we'd rather do that than watch a football game. I wanted to talk just a little bit about that—about the choices that people make in our culture, with so many options, so many different choices. We have the choice, for example, to take a walk in the forest, but instead will go to the gym and watch a sitcom on the treadmill. The exercise is the same, but the two experiences are vastly different.

D: Actually, my belief is that, if we're conscious and aware, we can develop our ability—our capacity—to love, in any situation. However, what you're talking about in regard to us not having time, and then you relating to being at the gym watching a sitcom, I think we use TV and spectator sports as a way to live vicariously. We're watching somebody else do something, we're watching somebody else have an experience. TV is one of the big ways we numb out. It is a way to avoid experience, rather than participate and involve ourselves in life. We're not conscious when we avoid experience in this way. And so I would say, in terms of time, we always have enough time to wake up and be conscious, and choose to have love, joy, and fulfillment in our lives.

B: Well, Diana, thanks for this commentary. It seems we both concur with what Suzie said, that pleasure is a great motivator. I hope we all can keep that in mind: that pleasure, higher consciousness, and transformative experiences are there for us, whenever we want them.

D: Yes, Bill, they are.

Chapter 8:

Living the Tantric Life

A conversation with husband and wife Bill and Melanie, whose union exemplifies the transformative power of tantra when integrated into daily life.

Diana: I'd like to introduce and welcome my very good friends, Melanie and Bill. Melanie is a book editor, graphic designer, and the co-producer of Tantra Talk Radio, the radio program I have been developing over the last four months. She is the most wonderful woman—giving and open and growing—so fun to be with and have as my friend. So thank you, Melanie, for being here.

Melanie: Thank you, Diana. It's wonderful to be with you here today.

D: And, Bill, I want to welcome you back to another interview. We have done many interviews in the last year, and I consider you a wonderful friend as well as an expert companion on this journey of growth, and on this commitment we both have to sacred sexuality education. I also deeply appreciate your expertise with over 30 years experience in the area of audio programming and sound engineering. Bill is the sound engineer for Tantra Talk Radio and editor and publisher of my upcoming book. Thank you so much for being here.

Bill: Well, it has been fantastic to be walking the tantra path with you, Diana.

D: And you, too, Bill. Now Melanie and Bill, you've been in a relationship now for how long?

M: We've been together 15 months and are now married.

D: And I'm curious, will you tell me what is your individual experience with sexuality in general, and then tantra in particular? I'm interested in any juicy tidbits you might want to share with me about sexual blocks. Many of us have been brought up in austere environments that have woefully limited our sexual growth. What is your sex history?

M: For me, Diana, like many women in our society, I had an early, very negative sexual experience against my will, at a young age, and grew up feeling a sense of self-loathing about that in regard to my sexuality. I am aware that as a young woman, I downplayed my sexuality, I didn't want to be attractive to men in a provocative way, and I can say it's true that I overcompensated with a self-protective attitude toward sexual attraction.

Through my twenties, and even my thirties, I had an experience of my own sexuality that was still injured, and I would say definitely curtailed. I did have, in my mid-thirties, a relationship that was very freeing. I had not studied tantra at that time, but there was a natural energetic between he and I that allowed me to actually begin to discover orgasm and orgasmic potential and allowed me to—really for the first time—enjoy sexuality, enjoy my body, enjoy the feeling of it and the desire for it. That was about eight years ago, and that relationship ended eventually. In the following years, I had a few relationships, but in them, never had met that level of sexual openness and fluidity that I had experienced earlier. Quite honestly, it was disappointing to me. I remember feeling, in one relationship in particular, that we had all these wonderful qualities as a couple going for us, but our sex life wasn't that great. So, I was going to settle for that, yet I could not forget the incredible sexual experience that I'd had and really longed for it again.

I didn't find that richness and depth of sexuality again until I met Bill. Immediately, from the very first times we were together sexually, I found a deep meeting, a connection, an energetic opening that was there and natural to us, that allowed me to access that same quality, that same depth of sexual openness and arousal, and orgasm in ecstasy. Now, Bill and I built up to these high levels. It took some time, but it was very evident in the beginning that there was a very special sexual chemistry between us. And this has brought to me for the first time a tantric practice and a tantric lifestyle.

D: Thank you so much for your sharing, Melanie. I'm impressed with your growth and your openness over time in light of that early experience that was so limiting. May I ask you, were you sexually abused?

M: Yes, I was. I was six years old.

D: Oh, I'm sorry. It sounds like you've really overcome that, and at the same time I appreciate hearing both the amount of pain and the way that your sexuality was repressed as a result of that experience. It's pretty common, which is why I wanted to ask you specifically what had happened because I think that you're a testimonial for all people, women especially, who have been sexually abused and who have struggled with their sexuality. There's so much fear around sexuality when that happens, especially at such an early age, so I think that your story is a wonderful inspiration for people who have had that experience, who are longing for the openness and connection a fulfilling sexual experience can bring.

M: Thank you. What I can say, from my own experience, is that my willingness and the support that I have had from Bill, who is a wonderful, loving, caring partner, has been the greatest blessing. I think that allowed me to be quite willing to let go of what had been binding me sexually, and gradually, increasingly, embrace more and more of what was there in my experience, in my capacity for pleasure, ecstasy, and union. I think if there's a willingness, love and sexual energy can be tremendously transformative.

D: And what have you done to study tantra? I'd be interested in what background you have in learning about tantra and applying it to your life and to your relationship with Bill.

M: My real learning of tantra, again, has been very recent. Bill and I have had a wonderful practice since early in our relationship of reading works by Margot Anand. In the evenings, we would take time to be together, to be very present with each other and share the day. One of the practices we began to include in that time is reading. One of us reads out loud, and we'll pause periodically to share what we experience from the material. This has been very helpful in learning, individually and as a couple, to apply new insights and wisdom to our lives in very real ways. We take the conceptual knowledge and bring it into our day-to-day experience. For example, we would discuss very precisely and literally aspects of our sexual experience in the context of something we had read in Margot's book just two days prior. I found that our sexual experience and the learned knowledge we were sharing were integrating more and more.

D: Oh, that's wonderful. Thank you, Melanie. Bill, will you tell us all about your background with sexuality in general?

B: Well, I got curious about it when I went through puberty. I began to see that there was a relationship between sexual arousal and altered states, which I experienced often after climaxing, and so I began to be very curious about that. I got married at an early age—at nineteen—and my wife and I were experimenting with this and we found it fascinating. At that time I was reading the Ananga Ranga and the Kama Sutra, some of the English translations of these far-Eastern texts. I have to mention that when I lived in Santa Fe in the mid-eighties, Margot Anand was my neighbor, she lived right down the street. I became friends with her as a neighbor, and we had a lot of informal chats. She was working on her first book at the time, and I thought boy, this is going to be a really good book. I'm still reading her books today with Melanie.

D: Fantastic. You have had experience with tantra from a very early age, then?

B: Yes, I would say so, though I didn't know they were tantric experiences when I was twelve or thirteen, but then later, being a curious scientist type, I started reading all the books about it. Everyone was saying at that time that the book to read about tantra was the Kama Sutra. When you actually read that kind of text, you realize that actually it's quite obscure and hard to understand. That's why the tantra pioneers, like Margot, were so helpful to me, because she could make ordinary sense of a western interpretation of these texts in a practical way. So that when they're talking about the multi-jewel lotus, they're actually talking about a woman's vagina. Then I realized, "Oh, that's what they're talking about." Back then in the sixties, sexual liberation was just starting and we were all just trying to figure it out.

D: Well, I have a question for both of you as a couple: Why did you decide to incorporate tantra into your relationship and what have the results been?

B: Well, I'll go first. I think it was very natural for us. As she and I became more intimate with each other, I began to realize that we were actually falling into a very sacred spiritual space. Then our contact, our touching, our sensuousness, and our love-making were all part of this very beautiful, wholesome picture of what I would call 'basic holding', the feeling of being fearless, of being fully secure in life. It was a natural evolution and, for example, when Melanie and I met, I was already working with you on this tantra series. When I told her about it she said, "Oh, that sounds fascinating, tell me more." So she was very open to it, and it was the beginning of our working together in these states. It fell in very naturally and seamlessly. I consider that to simply be a blessing, that's the only way I can explain it.

D: Wonderful. Melanie?

M: Yes, I agree with Bill that our tantric experience as a couple was very natural; it came very naturally to us. The learning of tantra came second, our tantra experiences being first. We had tantric experiences early on in our relationship and then began discussing what was happening and discussing it in the context of Margot's work and other areas of tantra teaching. As Bill said, he was working with you at the time, and I took great interest in the tantra philosophy and really enjoyed understanding it through my mind, but at the same time it was very definitely the case that Bill and I were having tantric experiences quite on our own.

In fact, many times it's been the case where I would have an experience during love-making—for example, feeling energy rise up through my central channel and explode through the top of my head—and then two or three weeks later, I'd read about it somewhere, very specifically describing my experience. This has happened time and again where we would have the experience first, and then I would come to intellectually understand it. And that's been my whole orientation to tantra; it has not been a process of reading books or going to workshops and trying to get there, it's actually been a process that has unfolded naturally through the experience of the love and the very beautiful—and I think rare—connection that Bill and I have.

D: And how old are you Melanie?

M: Just now forty-three.

D: And you've never been married?

M: No, I haven't.

D: OK. I'm asking because, again, I love that you're really opening to tantra in your forties. A person doesn't have to have been steeped in this since they were twenty or thirty; any age is fine to start this. For you, are there any experiences that you can share that, as you say, were naturally tantric, that you then discovered through your reading that were part of the tantric philosophy and lifestyle and practices. I love the one that you shared about the energy moving up and shooting out of your head. Are there others that you can think of, other specific sexual experiences that you would now consider tantric after your reading?

M: Yes. One particular example is the experience of having very different kinds of orgasm. For example, orgasm that arises or originates from my clitoris, as opposed to orgasm that arises from my inner vaginal channel or deeper inside, close to the cervix. I began to experience a widening variety of orgasms, and I hadn't ever learned or understood that there are these great varieties of orgasm. It was simply my experience, and I'm very aware that this is due to the openness I've had with Bill and the adventurous and exploring spirit that we both share.

D: In a workshop that I once participated in, we talked about the multiplicity of orgasmic experiences, and we laughed about how women can have ear orgasms or nose orgasms. Whatever the area of our body that is particularly sensitive can be a stimulus for orgasm, so our bodies are pretty wonderful. I think men are much more focused on their penis—their vajra or lingum, as we call it in tantric terminology—and yet women have so many triggers for pleasure.

M: It's true, so many triggers, so many places on and in our bodies. Another example of varieties of orgasm that I experienced before I learned about them, were an orgasm that was very localized, in a fairly small area of my body that was highly charged, and then another orgasm that was pervasive, very widespread, one that flowed through my whole being, spreading out all around me.

D: The Carter's define orgasm as "an involuntary re-distribution of energy". It sounds like you're again relating to many kinds of energetic experiences or energetic expressions that feel very orgasmic to you. I like that you're sharing this because it's validating and informative for women to know that there's no one right way.

In light of this, what would each of you share about what's been most enjoyable or fulfilling in your tantric experience and tantric practice together?

B: Well, first, I want to say something about Melanie's remark. One of the big insights I had as a young man was that if I was to have more of an orgasm, more of a climax throughout the body, that I actually had to consciously direct my energy away from the penis. You're right that men have a tendency to have concentrated climaxes and very short arousal times, but you also have some hydraulics involved, the fluid building up and being discharged. So I learned that if I really wanted to have a good time with my mate, the first thing I needed to do was redistribute that energy, and there's been a lot of books out there about how to contain the energy and slow the ejaculation process. I realized that the most powerful sexual organ is actually the brain, and that once I got my brain aligned with the fact that there's a whole zone there of arousal and excitement that sits below climax that you can hang out there, not only for minutes or hours but actually for days, and so perhaps that would be the answer to your question. One of the most enjoyable experiences I have with Melanie is that I can hang out in the space day after day with no goal, just enjoying the presence of pleasure.

D: So I'm curious, Bill—and men ask this a lot to me and in the workshops—is this painful for you to redistribute energy and not have an orgasm? Is it painful? Is it a loss? Does it feel less than enjoyable compared to the genital orgasm that men are used to every time they make love?

B: Well, I think the men's locker room term for that is 'blue balls', which states that if you make love with a woman and you don't climax, you're going to have this huge hydraulic store of seminal fluid in your scrotum and you're going to be uncomfortable. I never had that experience, actually. Being a scientist by nature, I realized that if you are a celibate man and you choose not to climax, not only if you choose not to have sex, but if you choose not to climax, the body actually starts to reabsorb the seminal fluid. So the notion of holding one's climax is, I believe, a myth. I always thought it was a way for men to get women to tolerate those climaxes. I never thought it had any medical truth. So, to answer your question, no, I never had pain or discomfort from not climaxing. Even as a young person where I used to climax two or three times a day, if I didn't do it for a few days I didn't experience any discomfort of any kind. What I did experience was an enlargement of pleasure, a way to match my energy with my mate. So I continue to enjoy that with Melanie, and because of our incredible compatibility and intimacy, it's now blossoming into a beautiful new way of love-making.

D: Would you say more about the enlargement of your capacity for pleasure in regard to what you've discovered through redistributing your energy and opening to prolonged orgasmic experiences?

B: I would call them eroticized states where the feeling of arousal, the tingle of arousal, spreads from the genital area, up into the torso, and into the hands and feet. I often experience this when Melanie is climaxing, and her orgasm is shooting up through her central channel into her head. I'm riding that wave, I'm right there surfing it with her, and not only does that cause me to feel like I'm a full participant, but I also get to experience all that energy. It's like I get to be there too. I know that some men feel like spectators when their partner is having multiple orgasms, but with Melanie, I've not been a spectator, I've been a full participant. I'm very present with her when she's having those experiences. So I would say being in the moment has been really wonderful with Melanie.

D: How great, thank you so much for sharing. Melanie, what has been most enjoyable and fulfilling for you in your practice of tantra as a couple?

M: A number of things immediately come to mind. I

think most profound has been this experience of discovery, of discovering how vast the female body is in terms of the pleasure and personal transformation that can be experienced—the ecstasy, the opening, the dematerializing of all the forms and ideas of who I am, moving through painful memories, feeling the structure of my personality dissolve and feeling instead a merging and a true spiritual connection with Bill. We have risen to these levels again and again in a variety of ways, and the variety itself has been very exciting to me. I often feel like I'm exploring a new world, and for me, in fact, it does feel like a new world. So, this is particularly wonderful in our tantric practice, the sense of co-exploration and discovery and the willingness to go to new places. Something that enhances this even further is the wonderful communication we have throughout our sexual experience. We're lovers and buddies, equally. We have a real, natural comfort in talking about very specific details about what we're experiencing, both at the physical level, emotional level, and also spiritually.

D: Thank you for that sharing. Again, I experience you as a testimonial to the beauty and the wonderful quality of understanding what this process is about, as well as experiencing it very richly. You seem to me to be going for, not only the experience, but the understanding which we talk about a lot in sacred sexuality education, that as you can name the experience, identify it, describe it, you then actually enhance it, you're able to expand that pleasure through your actual understanding of it. So, in the work I do as a sacred sexuality educator and a sex therapist, I ask people to name their experience and then expand it when it's a positive experience, so that they can not only repeat it, but so that their experience is enhanced. I really like that you're doing this, the two of you, and I really hear the pleasure and the bliss that you're having. It's like you're on this adventure of discovering new territory and having so much fun and being so in love and enjoying every step.

M: It' really interesting that you say that, Diana. A practice that Bill and I have just naturally fallen into is that in the after glow of our love-making, we lie quietly and absorb and enjoy feeling bathed in the feelings that we're experiencing. At some point Bill will say, "Tell me about your orgasms," and I'll describe what I experienced in detail. I didn't see this initially, but I see very clearly now that it has actually grounded me in my own orgasmic experience and allowed me to keep it, as you said, very much for it to not just have been something that I moved through and experienced and now it's gone. Describing my experience is a way of deepening it, enjoying it more, and understanding it more.

D: The other thing is, when you can be so specific with your partner, you give him an understanding, along with yourself, of what's happening which he can then use to deepen his connection with you, his understanding of how you work, of your process—not to repeat it, because it's not that he has a button to push now to turn you on. It's that the communication and your mutual understanding of each other enhances your pleasure physically and emotionally.

M: I also find that it enhances our intimacy and our connection as lovers, as human beings, and as partners. It reaches all those areas, the intimacy itself is nurtured through speaking, sometimes during love-making, always afterward. Sharing with each other very openly is part of this co-discovery process I feel. I will say that I feel grateful that I didn't begin the tantric path by going to workshops and learning techniques and trying them out. What Bill and I have done, I think, is we've found our own language with each other, we've discovered our own natural way of exploring ourselves and exploring each other, and there is very much a sense of an entity that's us, our couple-ness, who is leading this process. And we both surrender to it. We're not approaching love-making with methods or goals, and I feel that we're very freed up because of that.

D: Again, I love what you're saying because it relates to something that I think is a misunderstanding about tantra, which is that there are these techniques that will get people to this high state of multi-orgasmic response or of extended orgasm. I love your testimonial about how it's not the technique, it's the energy between the two of you and the process of your hearts opening and bodies connecting and spirits merging that really is creating this wave that is actually bigger than both of you, that directs you and opens you to higher and higher states of bliss.

M: Yes, very much, and there have been these beautiful breakthroughs along the way; when, for example, I first began to look at him eye-to-eye while we were making love. I remember initially it being a very raw experience of feeling exposed and a bit fearful; now when I look into his eyes and he is inside of me and we're making love, I feel the whole experience is increased, not only in the pleasure but in that feeling of connection, that feeling of unifying our energies and loving each other. There's a very strong quality of love that penetrates our sexual relationship, and that's very much a part of our being together sexually—it really is a physical expression of love. We often share with each other during our love-making how our heart feels.

D: I'm really getting the vulnerability that you and Bill are expressing to each other and actually experiencing. It seems to me that there's an opening up of your heart on a deeper and deeper level that is helping you develop that sense of merging.

To me, you're taking a risk to reveal yourselves by not only taking your clothes off with each other, but by opening up your hearts and sharing. In the idea of relationship being a spiritual path, I talk a lot about how you open up and see whatever's there, the fears or the feeling of inadequacy, the confusion— name it, express it, dissolve it, resolve it, and then go deeper. Does that fit your experience?

M: Yes. And there is a deeper meaning that takes place in going to these new and sometimes scary places. Bill hasn't had the fear or inhibition that I've experienced in that way; he's very open and very sexually healthy. I think that has allowed me to move beyond my own limitations of feeling a need to protect myself, or to fear that the exposure, the intimacy, is unsafe. I'm sure that's something a lot of women, and some men experience, that feeling of not being safe, of being in danger, the act of opening yourself up to someone, letting them see you for who you are, putting yourself up for any kind of judgment, and really being seen. As Bill and I have come together in our intimacy and in our love for each other, there has been this very natural falling away of the feeling that I need to protect myself. There's been a beautiful transformation from those little fears and doubts and insecurities in my sexuality, to this feeling of discovery that is actually fun and exciting and something I openly embrace.

D: Thank you so much. Bill, any comments in regard to all that Melanie has shared? I'm particularly interested in her comment that she hasn't experienced you having fears or vulnerabilities, that she considers you as having a really healthy sexuality.

B: I think that's a part of me that is pretty healthy. I got into psychotherapy pretty early in life because I realized that my parents were kind of different than a lot of parents—they were foreign born, they'd gone through the holocaust in the Second World War, they were living now in a foreign country. So I started therapy in my early twenties, and one of the things that my first therapist said to me, a woman, she said "You know what, Bill, one of the reasons you may be feeling strong and healthy sexually is 1) you didn't have any sexual abuse, and 2) all the trauma that took place in your life was before puberty, and so you don't associate sexuality with trauma, quite the opposite." The first young woman I was in love with—I didn't have sex with her but I was in love with her—she and I went into all these golden states of consciousness together. I was in the eighth or ninth grade. Later, I ended up marrying my high school sweetheart. So I have repeatedly experienced very, very positive associations with intimacy, and I've appreciated the relationship between emotional intimacy and physical intimacy. I've never made love to someone I didn't love, and frankly, some of the behaviors of men and women objectifying the other sex doesn't make any sense to me. I just don't know what they're talking about. I understand the concept, but I have no direct experience.

D: So, as a man do you have times where you feel vulnerable or have fears or inadequacies or confusion at all in your sexual relationship with Melanie?

B: I would say, the way it shows up is in the power of the sexual energy to expose rigidities in my personality, and so a lot of fear comes up as a result of that. I wouldn't say it's brought up as sexual trauma, it's brought up as general life trauma. As my tantric practice deepens and my sense of the basic goodness of being alive expands, it challenges all my little sacred fears.

D: That's what I was going to ask you in my next question. If there's any stumbling block that you've discovered on this tantric journey that we are on, what would you say it is?

B: I would say that I've discovered what I need to have for myself. I've seen this over and over again: the deeper you go, the more subtle the resistance is. So in the beginning, there's big old blaring obvious things, but when you get past that you're pretty comfortable and then you get into the more gnarly, more subtle rigidities, resistances, reactivities, and then you have to work those. So the answer to your question, yes, that's the challenge, but there's a reward. Each time I integrate, or digest this next stumbling block, then not only am I closer to Melanie because she's been a vehicle for working with that, but I'm actually more intimate with myself and an inner transformation has evolved.

D: What is a real life example of this?

B: Well, my mom passed away recently.

D: I'm sorry to hear that.

B: Thank you. I was expecting to experience the normal grief or loss, but instead I had repeated experiences of being abandoned by her. I didn't have that much of a relationship with her, it was painful actually, and so her passing brought up all the times she wasn't there for me. My openness with Melanie made me feel this much more acutely. There was no place to hide, and I didn't feel comfortable talking about my mother's death with anybody because I felt like I had socially inappropriate feelings, I didn't have the feelings of loss, I had feelings of relief, and feelings of deep disturbance. I found that if you're in a very intimate, highly communicative relationship with your Beloved, then you've got to face all those feelings. It's only over the last few months that that's happened to me.

D: I love your sharing this. It seems to me that when

you are willing to accept and love and respect yourself with any experience you have and when you give this to your partner as well, you are living relationship as spiritual path. The partnership simply allows you to go into the experience and feel it, resolve it, and allow the Beloved Divine Source of all that is to be there for healing as well. So I again appreciate your willingness to share this because it's so much what we're living and what we're wanting to communicate to others about what tantra can be.

B: I have a spiritual teacher, who's not a tantra teacher but does other type of work, and one of the things he said to me about my mother's passing was "Well, it got a very similar reaction as you did to your father's passing. Basically what is happening is you cannot fool yourself anymore about that parent. That parent is not going to transform on their deathbed, become a loving person, become the person you always wanted." So all this came up for me again. I had experienced this with my dad, and more recently with my mom, and to me, that's part of the tantric path, to be that exposed to the point where no one helps me work this out as much as Melanie. Even though I've got a teacher formally helping me, she's living with me and is there all the time.

D: Melanie, would you say anything about the blocks to consciousness that you've discovered through your tantric practice?

M: One of the stumbling blocks in particular for me is overcoming an attitude that was thrust upon me by my mother who was very bitter after the divorce of her and my father. She didn't choose to be divorced so she felt very betrayed. She was angry at him for many, many years. What I've been seeing in recent months is how that has penetrated my own way of being, not just in my relationships, but in my reticence to connect to another person. There is this attitude that bad things will happen if I trust someone or get too close. I generally felt unsafe in being exposed or in committing to a person and opening my heart to them. Growing up, I did not have a close-knit family experience. My divorced mother struggled to raise my brother and me. What brought us together was surviving, not loving or playing or celebrating or going on vacation. I remember through my early adult years feeling the sense that I wasn't like other people who are family types and who experience at least some measure of connection with one another. I wanted that so badly, that feeling of belonging, of family, and the loyalty and support that that brings. This is something now that has been exposed in numerous dimensions of itself with Bill. I see it transforming, and it's a beautiful experience.

D: I am feeling more and more appreciative of how you use your tantric practice as a spiritual path in your overall life, and so the next question would be, how are you integrating your tantric commitment and tantric practices into your everyday life?

M: One way that I would describe this is the way in which I feel during our love-making. I feel myself breaking open and breaking free, and this spills over into my day, the following days and following weeks. I am beginning now to increasingly have greater aliveness during the day, in all kinds of things I do—washing dishes, making dinner, working at my computer, shopping at the grocery store—there are more moments of feeling alive in my body, feeling connected to myself, feeling aware of my experience, my feelings, thoughts and judgments. It seems to me that, to the degree there is this exposure with Bill, I'm becoming exposed to myself as well. I feel a greater self-awareness as a result of breaking through the limitations of my fear of intimacy or denial of pleasure. As I open more and more to feeling pleasure in my own body, I feel better overall, physically, emotionally, and psychologically. I am seeing a very direct correlation between permission to feel good and the state of my mind and being in my day-to-day life.

D: Suzie Heumann of Tantra.com talked to me recently about her commitment and vision to express more intense love in the world. Her statement comes to mind when you talk. I can see through your stories exactly how that happened.

M: I've become a very strong believer in Margot's teaching that tantra is about opening ourselves up, loving our self, and loving each other more. There's also this beautiful interaction between pleasure and love, between pleasure and my heart opening.

D: How wonderful, thank you. Bill, do you have anything to add about how you have integrated tantra into your everyday life?

B: I would say is that it's giving me a continuously better attitude about life. I'm viewing life with increasing optimism, and I've found that tantra has done that for me my whole life. Now I'm in this wonderful relationship with Melanie, and we have this exquisite practical day-to-day compatibility so I feel safer, I feel more optimistic, and I feel more creative. I don't know if I would be doing a project like this say ten or fifteen years ago, but I feel I've got a level of maturity around it where I can talk openly about these things, and I'm very gratified that we're both here with you today to talk about all this.

D: Thank you. Two more questions.

B: Okay.

D: One is, have you found that your tantric philosophy and practices have helped you resolve conflict in your relationship, and if so, how?

B: Well, I think if you're on the tantric path of pursuing

the Beloved, you're going to experience on a continuous basis, day to day, week to week, a dissolving of differences and an interest in reducing activities. For me, that experience of the reduction of that experience is in the integration of my everyday life. It's just fantastic because not only am I not reactive with Melanie, I'm not reactive with everybody as much. I can see emotional upset before it comes out of my mouth, before I have a temper tantrum, before I say something hurtful—I can feel it on its way. That doesn't mean I'm going to inhibit myself, but I have much more clarity about its original source.

D: And you see your Beloved as your friend?

B: Yes. I see my Beloved as my ally. We've been practicing our marriage vows, and one of them is to be each other's best friend and closest ally.

D: And so again, the commitment and intention that you keep coming back to are actually part of your marriage vows, as well as part of your tantric lifestyle. It's as if it provides a compass and a lighthouse for you to keep orienting back to the path that you really believe in and value.

B: And it's a lighthouse of joy. Let's become attracted to something that's ecstatic and joyful. What a wonderful way to live. I work in the media, making money over controversial or bad news, so it's so uplifting to have a path that's all about joy, tolerating joy, having that in you and enjoying.

D: Melanie, I was going to ask you a different question, what tantric pearl of wisdom would you have to share as a parting thought?

M: What comes to mind is that giving ourselves pleasure is far more than feeling good. There is a spiritual teaching that says you don't need to work to get enlightened, that state already exists in you, you just need to remove what's in the way of it. In other words, we all have a natural radiance, but we don't know it because we're so caught up in all of our thoughts, thoughts that filter how we see life, all the opinions, all the attitudes, judgments, likes, dislikes. What is so beautiful to me about the tantric path is that it takes us directly to experiences of our own essence, that pure radiance that we are. What I suspect is happening is that all the clutter that's blocking my experience and expression of my radiance, and of love itself, is dissolved in the beauty of the orgasmic and connective experiences that I have with Bill.

D: Beautiful. I want to thank you both, and I appreciate your year together preparing for your coming marriage, which will happen in two weeks. I see you as such conscious human beings individually, and such a beautiful couple who is a role model and example for all of us of living love, joyfully, consciously, blissfully. Best wishes to you both.

Chapter 9:

Seeds of Enlightenment

A conversation with Margot Anand about the sacred doorways tantra opens and how we can expand the spiritual dimension of our sexual experience.

Diana: Hello Margot, where are you calling from?

Margot: I'm just back home from a very wonderful journey, the best journey of my life. I went to Bhutan with friends, who are all into tantra, with a guide who has been to Bhutan ten times already. There I went back to the source of the SkyDancing tantra.

D: Oh, wonderful.

M: And I found there the last tantric kingdom on this Earth, actually. It was absolutely incredible to be in a kingdom where women are legally allowed to have several husbands and where men are legally allowed to have several wives. It's really great.

D: Fantastic, Margot. I knew you'd have many riches to share with us today.

M: It's a very different way of living life over there, which is why it's so interesting to go to all these countries. Bhutan is very impressive; it's very open. We met the queen, the king, and all the ministers—we were blessed to have these encounters. We also went to all the sacred places in the monasteries; these are normally not open to tourists, but we had special permits. We went to all the shrines with the sacred relics. And, boy, the transmissions were incredible. It was really powerful. I saw the most beautiful tantric art I've ever seen in my life. Of course they don't let you photograph once you go inside these places, but it was amazing to see. It was really, really a blessing.

D: The transmissions, Margot, what knowledge or wisdom was particularly important to you with the transmissions?

M: I would not know; it was energetic, it was magical. You enter into a place, and you get touched by an enormous energy, and your heart opens, and you have visions. And then you give offerings and you get blessed. For me personally, the knowledge was simply touching the source of my lineage and meeting with the places where Yeshe Sogyel was practicing riding the wave of bliss. I was reading about her biography while we traveled to the places where she got enlightened, which was really quite something.

D: Sounds wonderful. It sounds like you were empowered by this adventure.

M: Yes, I've been empowered lately to be really blissful in everyday life. That's really nice. [Laughter]

D: How magnificent! I'd like to ask, Margot, what is enlightenment? And how does our tantra path contribute to enlightenment?

M: Well, enlightenment begins and it never ends. The tantric path is basically giving you a lot of tools, and these tools have to be practiced over long periods of time. And each of them, in the practice of them, holds the seed of enlightenment. Like riding the wave of bliss, if you practice seven steps on a regular basis, or if you sit and meditate on a regular basis, or if you connect with one of the holders of the lineage—like Padma Sambhava, which I did, I went to the places where he meditated and sat there and received his transmission for sure—so you go as deep as you can with the people who are the holders of the lineage and much can happen.

D: So, would you say that it's a process? It's not that we arrive anywhere? One of the questions my clients will ask is, "Are we there yet?" How would you answer that question, Margot?

M: Well, you know that you're there—or more there than before—when you're more happy, because the state of happiness is a natural state given to us human beings. But when the self or the ego develops as you grow up, then you start to create duality and divisions: "That is good and that is bad," and, "I want this, and I don't want that." And then, all of a sudden, you can't accept what is, because you're fighting against it, you know? You're not in the surrender. Adyashanti defined enlightenment as surrendering to the inevitable. It's an interesting definition. I mean, all of a sudden, you learn (like Byron Katie says) to love what is—as opposed to thinking that you're only going to be happy if the picture of your life corresponds to what you want it to be or what you think it should look like.

So, one way of looking at this is, do you touch the mystery? The mystery is helping you to be present moment to moment, to what is arising without knowing what the next moment is going to bring. And the more you can be in that place, the more nourished you are, the more taken care of you are by existence, and the easier it gets. But, until we get to that place, we have to practice.

D: So it's not only a matter of practicing in our sexual encounters and raising the energy from our sexual chakra up to our crown center. It's practicing every moment, opening up with all of our chakras to the experience of ecstasy, even in the smallest moment—even in, say, riding in the bus or driving in the car.

M: If you practice every day, opening your chakras in a meditation, for instance, and then you sit quietly and you begin to open your chakras to receive from the universe. Because bliss is the ability to be able to receive; to really tune in with 'what is' through trust. And then you get to a point where there's a synchronicity, to where whatever you think manifests. You know, there's less and less distance between matter and thought, or between matter and spirit, and it's all a constant flow of manifestation. So, if you're in a moment where there is a blessing in your life, or you are able to receive the blessing, or tune into the gratitude of all the blessings that are abounding all around, then you begin to receive more gifts and more bliss and more flow. To do a meditation every day, to open up the chakras and then sit in a receptive mode, is a good thing because then it will allow you to tune in with spaciousness every moment—whatever you do.

D: Ah hah. I'm feeling spacious just listening.

M: I really hope to convey a little bit of all the wonderful presence that I got in Bhutan and elsewhere.

S: You are conveying it. [Laughter] What do you say, Margot, to the practitioner who sits in meditation and is distracted by worries of, "Am I doing it right? Is it working?

Am I being effective?" Many clients report difficulty with this issue.

M: Oh, I see. Well, it's good to go to a meditation group, where you get some tools, and then to go home and tune in with the tools—because the tools tune you back into the energy of the group, which is strong and solid. It's kind of like a morphogenetic field was created in the group, and then you can tune back into it. So, if we do the morning meditations like the Quantum Light Breath or the Kundalini, then you do them. There are instructions, it's guided. And then you find a place where you can let go of the questions of your mind, and you know, inside you know how to let go, you know how to be in the energy, you know to breathe and move, and then you don't worry about whether you're doing it right or not, because your body will guide you. And something that helps along those lines is the five movements of Gabrielle Roth, because they also help us in letting go of the mind, letting the body move, and enjoying that. That's a very supportive kind of practice, I would say.

D: It sounds to me, Margot, that it's a matter of discipline, or action and surrender. So we do our practices as best we can, in order to develop ourselves, and then we surrender into the moment and trust the process. Is that how you would describe it?

M: Yes, that would be it.

D: Margot, what about the kriyas that come up for us, the physical shaking and trembling from so much energy moving through us? How are we to explain this or deal with it? Sometimes they arise in the midst of our practice, and sometimes they happen when we're out in the world, in a public place. A friend was telling me recently that he was standing in line at a supermarket with his daughter, and he was feeling present and blissful, and he started to allow the physical trembling right there in line. He finally explained it to his twelve-year-old daughter, what was going on, what that was. He explained it to her as energy moving throughout his body, and she totally got it.

M: Beautiful. That's great. Well, children are very open to that. Children are much closer to enlightenment than we are, because they have less self in mind, and not specialization that have been put in their training. I was just listening to a conference yesterday, about a master in India who is interesting me. He was saying that children at his ashram were getting it the fastest, the awakened state. So, I mean, basically we all have it, it's just a matter of getting out of the way so we can enjoy what we've got. [Laughter] Sometimes we can do that better than others; some days we can do that better than other days.

D: I do the Inner Flute Meditation every day along with the P.C. Pump. I actually have just incorporated this into my meditation practice, and it's been wonderful, because I feel like I'm incorporating my body and the physical sensation of the first and second chakras with my third eye and my crown chakras. Then I create sacred space by setting my intention every day for how I want to live my life that day. I dedicate the energy of orgasm to manifesting my dreams. I'm really going forward into life, trusting myself, trusting the process, trusting my energy, and trusting my body as good and as a source of joy. So, it's been wonderful, and it's also been ordinary. Now I've been thinking about how to bring tantra energy, that energy that's so ecstatic, into even the ordinary moments.

M: Yes, well waking up gets you to a place where it's very ordinary and very extraordinary at the same time, and you can't even talk about it. It's just quite amazing, you know. You are in this blissful state, but you can't run over on the roof tops and say, "I'm blissful! I'm blissful! It's so great!" Bliss is actually a very ordinary thing, you know. Very humble, nothing special, and nothing to talk about.

D: That's helpful to know.

M: Yes! We're used to this idea that awakening and bliss is ten thousand stars and trumpets blasting, but it's not that. There's something very modest and humble and simple and ordinary about it.

D: Ahh, thank you for such a real response. [Laughter] Margot, recently I had an experience making love with a partner when we were not in a committed relationship. And I noticed that, because I got into some fear of, "Would I see this person again?" I didn't practice sacred space, and I didn't do my practices with the lovemaking. And the entire experience was a lot emptier, not as meaningful. So, I realize that it's important not to let go of the practices when I'm with someone who has not studied tantra. It takes walking my talk, regardless of the situation and taking the courage to practice wherever I am.

M: Yes, well I've noticed that even men who are not at all into SkyDancing Tantra, actually like it if you do a little ritual with them before you make love. It's kind of a teaching, or it's a mini transmission. And who is not going to be happy to receive something like that, you know?

D: Good point. What suggestions would you offer to keep ourselves on the path in light of the daily challenges of life? I think we all get into this place of, "Work takes a lot of time and energy. At the end of the day, I don't have the time or energy for my spiritual practice." Or I will create time at night to do some of my practices, and then people call or there's some other disruption or interruption.

M: Well, it's interesting because, by living in other cultures—as I do a lot, like living in France or Bali—I feel that

I have a more general perspective of context from which to look at the American culture. When we're in America, we all think we are completely in a trance. We are obsessed with thinking that reality works this way: that we have to get up and make to do lists, from morning to night, and that's life. We run from one thing to another, constantly distracting ourselves from our own experience.

But, in fact, it doesn't have to be like that. I lived for one month without any cell phone and hardly any communication—I was on my email only two times in one month, can you imagine? In completely different cultures, where I was busy doing ritual and watching nature, and doing spiritual and mystical things, my life went on when I came back here. Everything was the same as it was, nothing collapsed, bills got paid by someone else while I was gone. Everything moved along normal channels. My life was all the same as it was before.

So we're in this obsession that we can't leave our routines and lists, that bills and everything will fall apart. It's a total illusion, and we're caught in this illusion. There are many other ways of living, and there are many people—including Americans—who have chosen to live elsewhere, because they don't want this madness. I can take this madness for a while, but I can take it less and less often, I have to say.

D: So, taking time away is one thing. And even when I don't go away, I know for me, I've had to draw a black line through my calendar, and make it imperative that I don't schedule anything at certain times in my day. I give myself that as a spiritual practice—realizing that my ego's going to want to not pay attention to that, and schedule, schedule, schedule. But I need to keep committing to creating that sacred space. I see this as part of my spiritual path. It may not be the end result, and I may fall off the path at times, but to keep committing to what I really believe in is really important.

M: Yes. It's a two-edged sword because you can do it that way, and then you create an either/or and you say, "Well, this space is going to be empty space, and this space I have to keep protected, and this is this, and this is that." It's as though spaces are fighting with each other. Or you can cultivate spaciousness inside in such a way that you actually are always in touch with it, whatever you do—whether you go to the bank, whether you drive the car, whether you're talking to someone. There is always consciousness being aware of itself, or the witness watching what is going on. And there's always the knowledge that, in the background, behind the forefront of all the actors on the stage and the business happening in the background, there is the backstage, which is a very vast, cathedral-like area with consciousness, and it is just watching the show, where presence is always happening.

So, it's our mind that actually splits us, and it's our fears that create the tension. But it all really is an illusion. It's really self-created. And it's possible to stay spacious and present to the movie—whatever the movie may be. [Laughter] Of course, that's all the cultivation that we need to do through our meditation, or through our travels, or through lovemaking—through whatever we do. It's just to keep on drinking at the source, and cultivating presence to being.

D: What often happens—I hear my clients report this—is that we have all these 'shoulds' about tantra and the practices. "I should do this practice, and that practice, and the next practice, and read this, and do this, and do that." It is often difficult to really live the truth that I can practice as I walk in the woods, or I can practice as I take care of the dog, or clean the house, or do something else."

M: I went through a phase like that myself. I can relate. Better you do it like that than not do it at all. So you're already one up on your self, by just keeping time for the practice and being disciplined. That's important. For me, I'm not the disciplined kind. I could do the practices whole-heartedly for a certain amount of time, and then no matter how much I told myself, "I have to be disciplined and meditate every morning," forget it. I don't manage. So now, I make my life my meditation. And I know when I'm in alignment, when I'm in joy, and when I'm not. When we're in joy, we simply surrender to the inevitable—which is life lived, through us. The benchmark, as far as I'm concerned, is happiness. So, if we feel happy, then we got it. It's working. And if we don't feel happy, we have to re-examine what's happening.

D: What about that, Margot? In the moment, how can I open simply to 'what is', and keep loving?

M: Well, as long as your happiness is conditional, as long as it's dependent upon something outside of yourself, that's not the true happiness. As long as your happiness depends on a having, rather than a being, then it's a trap; because you have to consume something—a boyfriend, a penis, a new dress, a spa treatment, a trip—I'm the trip consumer myself. We all do that. But there is another kind of happiness that is growing, which is just the happiness for no reason—the happiness that is gratitude. Can you imagine? Have you ever been to the doctor, sat down before an examination, and had to fill a sheet of paper by putting your check mark in all the different illnesses have you had? Answer, have you had surgery? Have you had diabetes? Have you had a bladder infection? Have you had a broken limb? Have you had pneumonia? Have you ever had to do that? I'm sure you have, right?

D: Sure.

M: Well, don't you have a moment of total gratitude when you don't have to check any of these things, and you suddenly realize how incredibly healthy you are? I certainly do. I feel such a gratitude right there. I'm alive, I'm healthy, I'm strong, my body functions, my mind is clear. Wow, just that. I have a vehicle through which I can wake up, and I am waking up—we all are. Sometimes I could just get up and jump up and down with gratitude. I mean, watch the dogs in the street. Can you imagine that you're reborn as a dog? Some of the dogs here have it good. But some of the dogs don't have it so good, you know? So it's a very interesting and powerful thing just to have gratitude for what we have.

D: So, to cultivate happiness, but not to clutch to it.

M: That's right. Yes, that's exactly it.

D: It sounds simple, but not easy to do it seems.

M: It's so easy! We already have it.

D: Oh! [Laughter]

M: Maybe we have to do a laughing meditation when we get up. [Laughter] Oh, boy.

D: Well, many spiritual teachers and meditation masters say what you just said: already having it, already being enlightened, already being happy. They often talk about the tricky nature of the mind and seeing through that. They also emphasize technique, and not to be attached to technique in the process, because that's dualistic. A dualistic approach in which you pick something up because you think it's going to lead you somewhere. So I'm concerned with that, I'm aware of that when I take a tantric practice. I think it's important to be aware of that.

M: Well, let's look at it for a moment. For example, what are you going to say about breathing? Breathing is something that is absolutely fundamental to staying alive, right? Now, are you going to say that breathing is a technique? Well, yes and no. Breathing is something that happens spontaneously, and you can turn it into a practice or a technique, because you can refine it, you can prolong it, you can hold it. There are four stages to breathing, and practicing that gives you a shortcut to entering into spaciousness beyond the mind. I would consider this to be a good practice, because it simply helps you to cultivate something that you already have and remember that it's there.

So you pay attention to it, because the voice of truth and the face of bliss are two things that are very discreet. They manifest on a regular basis, but if you don't know how to pay attention and be there with it, you miss it. Or you don't give it the value that it really has, or you're too busy making to-do lists to really listen to that small, still voice that is pointing to the right direction. And it may be a direction you don't really want to look into. So, practices are cool if they get us to a place that is nourishing for the soul, for the spirit, and allow us to cultivate the well-being and the balance of emptiness in everything we do.

In practices of longevity, there are certain exercises that are done by masters where they breathe and meditate in such a way that they don't need to eat or even drink. I did that at some point in my life, so I know it's true. The old masters in the Himalayas had mastered that so that they could be in retreat in caves, and they didn't need to eat anything, they didn't need to breathe, because they were receiving their nourishment from prana and from sunlight. So this particular mastery is what wandering the Himalayas is about, and to rise into a cave, and to find there a person that presumably had been sitting there for 600 years in complete stillness and meditation, almost like a piece of rock. But ourselves, we don't want to have this attitude, "Well I just want to sit here until I get enlightened, because I'm afraid that if I die, then I'm going to miss the possibility of fully waking up." We don't need to sit for 600 years, we already have it.

D: Ah, yes.

M: So it's amazing what you find. Everybody adjusts according to their benchmark their particular idea of what it is, you know?

D: Is that kind of experience part of the tantric lineage? That kind of longevity experience? Not eating, for example?

M: You know, that's part of something that's always interested me, the possibility of surviving without food—and I've done it for 45 days, and for one week without drinking liquid. And I definitely believe it's possible, but it requires a different lifestyle than what we have here in the states. The tantric lineage is a vast one, and some tantra masters have gone through total austerities, living in caves, not eating, practicing mantras, doing three-year retreats with practices all day long. There are all sort of things that go with it. There is a mystical dimension of tantra that I have yet to teach really fully—which I will, sooner or later, dare to step into and teach.

D: Fascinating, you always keep us on our toes, Margot.

M: Yes, and me too!

D: Before we end our conversation, Margot, do you have any closing comments?

M: Ah, yes. I would love to talk a bit about something dear to my heart. In my travels, I have found that there are some countries where they declare a National Day of Orgasm. That's a day when people are supposed to stay home and make love. [Laughter]

D: Really?

M: I'm serious! The king of Bhutan declared that there was one more important thing than the consideration about National Gross Product, and that is National Gross Happiness.

And that idea of National Gross Happiness was the upper-most important value at the court of the king and in the government. Then the idea got picked up by the United Nations, and now they have symposia in several countries of the world with specialists on ecology and economy, and they're talking about, "How could we bring about National Gross Happiness? How would that look?" So a few of us went there, and our idea is to bring that to the United Nations, so that they can declare a week of National Happiness in every country of the world.

D: I love that, Margot. It's a wonderful way of ending our talk today, to be talking about National Gross Happiness. I would add to that, "How can we create that in our own lives?"

M: Yes, it is something each of us can do, not just for a day or a week, but for every day. It's a choice we have.

D: That is so inspiring, Margot. Thank you so much for your time today. I am so grateful. And Margot, will you share your website address?

M: Yes, it's www.MargotAnand.com. I've just written an article about the Bhutanese adventure and the magical mystery tour. I'm turning that into a journal, which I'm doing for the whole ten people on the journey. I'm going to add pictures, and I'll be putting that on my website. It should be there by fall of 2005.

D: Wonderful. Thank you, thank you.

M: Thank you, Diana.

Interview Commentary with Diana and Bill

Bill: Diana, I had a couple of questions about tantra practices. What are yoni healings? Tell us a little about that.

Diana: Yoni healing is the G-spot work, where it's actually focused on the G-spot. And then, also, the whole inside cavity of the vagina, or yoni in Sanskrit. It means 'sacred space.' Margot and many Tantric practitioners talk about the yoni because it creates more of a sacred sense of reverence for the genitals. And the yoni healing is work with the G-spot, to both stimulate the G-spot and explore by palpating, with the fingers, the area of the G-spot. And so often, people hold a lot of wounding in that area that has never been even acknowledged or understood, much less released. So what happens with yoni healing, is that the partner inserts his finger into her yoni and explores the area of the yoni, and especially the G-spot. With that particular stimulation, usually, people experience pleasure. And there's also a heightening of energy, and a strong release of energy.

Different people have many, many different experiences. They can... One of my friends ended up having a lot of grief. She also had flashbacks of the birth of her second child, and labor, and delivery, and the pain around that. And she didn't even know that she was holding pain until that release work happened. And then, from there, she felt a big relief, and release, and freedom, and lightness, and a lot more pleasure. So when people have the experience of yoni healing—when women do—they can release a lot of old negative feelings, pent up feelings, sadness, hurt, anger, fear, and then leave room for more pleasure. It's just like any other organ of the body: as it's exercised, as it's developed, it becomes stronger to experience and hold pleasure.

B: Well, David Deida, in his new book on sexuality writes about the G-spot orgasm as being a more subtle and a deeper orgasm. Would you comment on that?

D: Well, there's many, many orgasms that people have. And

the G-spot orgasm is simply—the way I describe what people mean when they say a G-spot orgasm—is it's stimulation of the G-spot that then brings people to orgasm, just like you have stimulation of the clitoris or stimulation of the entire vaginal barrel, or the nipples on the breast of a woman, or the vajra (or penis) for a man. So the orgasm, yes, is deeper, because the G-spot is located inside the woman. So the experience of pleasure seems to be more internal than external. With some women, and, again, I don't think there's any one particular experience that is called "the experience": each woman, especially, is very unique and will have her own unique experience. And some women don't have G-spot orgasms, but those that do report internal pleasure, deeper, and, yes, more subtle. And at the same time, there can be a release of fluid from the G-spot orgasm that is called 'amrita'—A-M-R-I-T-A.

B: And, anatomically, it's the same group of nerve bundles that lives in the clitoris. In other words, it's the same set of nerve bundles as actually going down the vaginal barrel. That's what I learned in school.

D: Right. And the way to locate it is to, if a woman is lying on her back and her partner puts his finger with the finger nail down, so the palm is facing up, and inserts his forefinger into the woman and then presses up and forward... So it's at the top and front part of the vaginal barrel. When the partner presses up and forward like he's hooking his finger, he can usually find a little area—it's about the size of a nickel—that has bumpiness to it. It's a little rougher than the rest of the vaginal area is. It's rougher and it is small, and is pretty easily located. And when that is palpated or stimulated, it brings a lot of pleasure and emotion to a woman.

B: Hmm. Thanks for the clarification. The other question I have refers to a term that was referred to as 'Quantum

Light Breath'. Could you tell us a little bit about 'Quantum Light Breath'?

D: Actually, this is a breathing practice that is very much like Holotropic Breath Work or rebirthing breath work. It's a CD that was developed several years ago to music. The idea is to breathe twice as fast and twice as deep for an hour. The facilitators direct people as to how to breathe and offers them certain suggestions for imagery. He encourages people to let go of thinking. And just go into the music. There is a progression to the music which, at first, is very earthy and rhythmic, and then gets more ethereal and transcendental, and finally very meditative and relaxed. And the breathing lasts for about an hour. People are encouraged to be blind folded, and to either sit or lie down, and then to let the rhythm of the music—as well as the breath itself—lead them into whatever expression, emotionally and verbally and physically, wants to come out. What happens, again, is the breath work bypasses the mind and the thinking.

And so, whatever needs to come up for a person, on an emotional level—it can be history from the past, it can be past life experiences, it can be present emotional experiences that people are having, it can be physical experiences... So, whatever needs to happen, it's like the inner wisdom of each person gravitates towards healing. If left on our own, we will heal ourselves, because we have a natural tendency to heal. And that's the same for the physical, as well as the emotional, body. So our emotions as well as our soul gets really accessed, and expressed, and healed through this process.

B: Well, it does remind me very much, of the Holotropic Breath Work developed by Stan Grof. Another question that came up for me was how to deal with the daily challenges of life and do your Tantra practice. I wonder what you might have for our readers, in terms of what to do about that challenge?

D: Well I really loved that focus in our discussion, because it reinforces the idea that Tantra is not just about sex; it is a spiritual path. And sexual energy is used to heighten our overall energy, so we can then experience ourselves fully. And, at the same time, love making experiences end. And we then get to look at the question, "What is life?" after orgasm without the beloved. And I think that's what Margot was talking about, that the Tantra path gives us a template of what is bliss, and what is happiness—high-level happiness.

And what does our body feel like when we're in bliss? I like to think about bliss as an open hand that is totally receptive and highly sensitive to the experience of being touched and being connected to with someone or something in every moment; versus a closed fist. A closed fist is a closed system with no access to the environment around it, and there's a lot of tension that happens with a closed fist. So the idea is to really let go of expectations, that our life be any certain way and to follow our bliss—like Joseph Campbell says.

But, I think the discussion was focused on cultivating happiness but not clinging to it, and not even pursuing it. Just listening to our truth about what does happiness look like? How do I feel physically, emotionally, mentally, and spiritually when I'm happy? And what contributes to my happiness? Then how do we cultivate it, move towards it? Margot has said, for her happiness, she really loves taking time away from the business of her life, and really sitting in meditation, and opening, and receiving inner wisdom. And from that place of openness and relaxation, she really is committing to seeing divinity, seeing the Beloved, seeing happiness in every moment. I was doing the same thing yesterday at the airport. I was thinking about, "What is happiness, what is bliss?" I was coming back from a trip from Colorado. And so, happiness to me yesterday was looking at the back of a lady walking in front of me, and seeing her conversation with her husband, and appreciating their interaction; and listening to the flop-flop of her shoes; and thinking, "That's a neat sound." And liking her hair-do, and the colors of her outfit....

And so, opening with my senses to being in that moment, and feeling quiet in my body and my being, and receptive to what is in this moment. And as I say that, I think, "Gosh, so what about pain? When people are going through tragedies?" And what I would say about that is, "So that's there too. Life brings us that." And to open to that as well, to simply keep opening with deep acceptance of what is. And also deep curiosity. So what is this that's coming up? And how can I accept this? And how can I learn more about who I am in this space? So all of that is contact with my Beloved, the Beloved moment, being who I am as my own Beloved, and then whoever... what my Beloved is in this moment—it could be the man at the grocery store.

B: Interesting. Well, Diana, I have one final question, and that's a commentary on Margot's suggestion—which I just love—a National Day of Orgasm.

D: Isn't that great? And the National Gross Happiness level. So the National Day of Orgasm and the National Gross Happiness level, instead of the National Gross Product. So orgasm is—if you recall our discussion with Steve and Lokita Carter—an involuntary distribution, redistribution, of energy. So orgasm can be a laugh—Margot loves just laughing, and started that sharing on our call. So to look at, "How can we be orgasmic? And how can we dedicate our lives to orgasm?

To being open and pleasure filled, and love filled, and joyful, every moment? How can we belly laugh? How can we breathe deeply? How can we go barefoot? How can we be naked and eat grapes?" So that we look at the path of tantra as a path to bliss, and bring bliss into our daily lives.

B: Well I remember Steve Carter talking about how even a yawn is an orgasm, so I propose that we have that National Day of Orgasm. And perhaps the Postal Service can put out a commemorative stamp—I think that would really remind people of their own joy.

D: [laughter] That's wonderful, Bill. I love that.

B: Thanks so much for this wonderful conversation and this wonderful commentary.

D: Oh, thank you for your wonderful, thought filled questions! I love them, and I so enjoy deepening the experience of our sharing with Margot, so thank you for helping that happen, Bill. It's good as usual.

B: Yes!

Appendix

Expressing Anger Constructively

The following is an excellent model of expressing anger constructively. It is based on the 3 stages of anger. The 1st stage is the fiery stage of anger where our energy for fighting and striking out at the other is very strong. Many times, this is when we say and do things we regret later. This is a good time to take a time out, be alone and center ourselves. During this time, we can express our energy physically through screaming, crying, pounding on a pillow, hitting a punching bag or getting physical exercise. The focus here is getting the energy out and understanding what our deep feelings and needs are. Writing a letter not to be sent to the person we are angry at, but using it to express our feelings and understand our needs and learn how to take responsibility to get our needs met is the point of this letter. The following is a format for the letter:

Dear_____,
I'm angry about ....
I'm sad/ hurt about ....
I'm afraid of ....
What I regret is ....
What I deserved then and now is ....
What I appreciate about me, about you is ....
What I want now is ....
What I'm willing to do to get what I want is....
What I'm learning about myself from this situation is ....
Love,
Me

Write an ideal response letter from the person you are upset with. Two things happen when you do this. You nurture yourself with hearing what you want to hear from the other person (the right brain where emotional healing happens doesn't know the difference between imagination and reality). Also, you get clear about what you really want from the other person. You can then communicate much more clearly to the other person what it is you want.

The 2nd stage of constructive anger management is to communicate what you are feeling and what you need. The way to do this is to take the letter that you wrote and re-write it in a caring way so that you can share your feelings with your partner in a way they can hear and receive. This is also an important time to plan how this will not happen again and to agree on changes each of you will make for prevention. Once each person acknowledges how they will act to prevent this happening in the future, the way is paved for an apology, forgiveness and gratitude.

The 3rd stage is making up. This is a time for cuddling, holding each other, re-establishing the closeness that was lost. It also can be an important time to share gratitude for having gotten through a rough time and gratitude for your beloved partner.

Bibliography

A.H. Almaas. Various works. www.ridhwan.org.

Anand, Margot. *The Art of Everyday Ecstasy*, Broadway Books, New York, NY, 1998.

Anand, Margot. *The Art of Sexual Ecstasy*, Jeremy P. Tarcher, Los Angeles, CA, 1989.

Anand, Margot. *Sexual Ecstasy, The Art of Orgasm, Exercises from the Art of Sexual Magic*, Jeremy P. Tarcher/Putnam, New York, NY, 2000.

Anand, Margot. *The Sexual Ecstasy Workbook, The Path of Sky Dancing Tantra*, Jeremy P. Tarcher/Putnam, 2005.

Foley, Sallie; Kope, Sally A; Sugrue, Dennis P. *Sex Matters For Women*, The Guilford Press, New York, NY, 2002.

Heumann, Suzie and Campbell, Susan. *The Everything Great Sex Book*, Adams Media, Avon, Massachusetts, 2004.

Judith, Anodea and Vega, Selene. *The Sevenfold Journey, Reclaiming Mind, Body & Spirit Through the Chakras*, The Crossing Press, Freedom, CA, 1993.

Kuriansky, Dr. Judy. *The Complete Idiot's Guide to Tantric Sex*, Alpha Books, Indianapolis, IN, 2002.

Richardson, Diana. *Tantric Orgasm for Women*, Destiny Books, Rochester, VT, 2004.

Williamson, Marianne. *Illuminated Prayers*, Simon & Schuster, New York, NY, 1997.

Yarian, David. Various works. www.DavidYarian.com

Zilbergeld, Bernie. *Male Sexuality*, Bantam Books, New York, NY, 1981.

Zilbergeld, Bernie. *The New Male Sexuality*, Bantam Books, New York, NY, 1993.

VIDEOS

Margot Anand's *Secret Keys to the Ultimate Love Life* (DVD Trilogy)

Margot Anand's *The Art of Orgasm For Men & Women* (2-DVD Set)

Tantric Yoga for Lovers by Steve and Lokita Carter

The Breath of Tantric Love with Steve and Lokita Carter

Tantric Massage for Lovers with Steve and Lokita Carter

To purchase any of these videos, visit www.tantra.com.

List of Diagrams

THE 7 CHAKRA ENERGY CENTERS

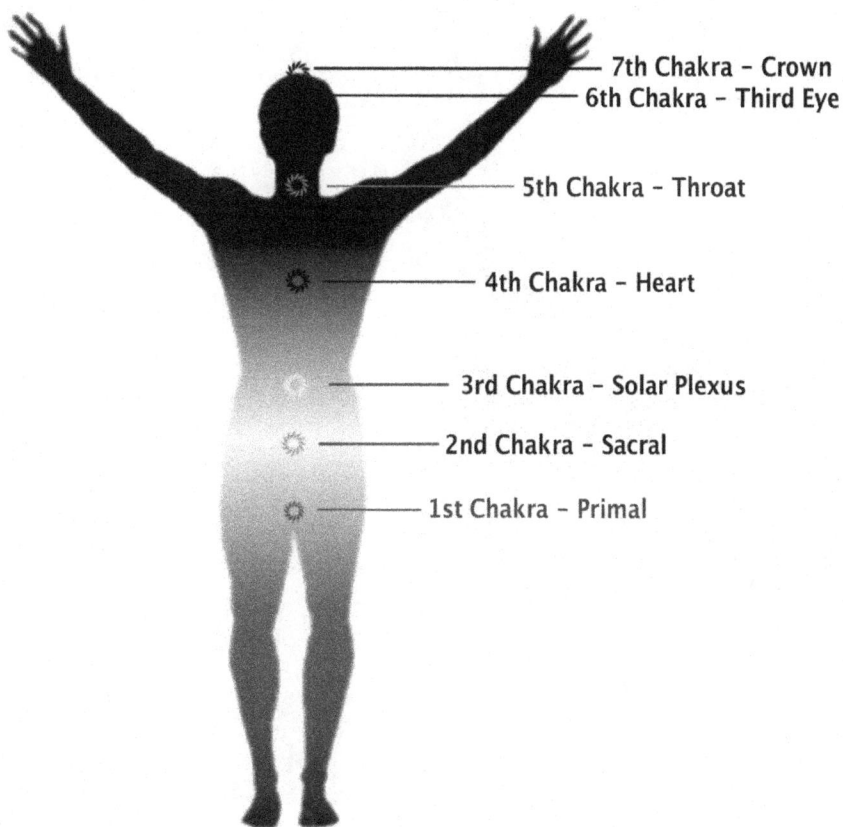

7th Chakra - Crown
6th Chakra - Third Eye

5th Chakra - Throat

4th Chakra - Heart

3rd Chakra - Solar Plexus

2nd Chakra - Sacral

1st Chakra - Primal

The Seven Chakras

CHAKRA	LOCATION IN BODY	COLOR	FUNCTION	POSITIVE & NEGATIVE QUALITY	AFFIRMATION	MANTRA
FIRST: Root, Primal, Base	Base of spine, Pelvic floor, Legs & feet, Genitals, (penis, vagina, clitoris, & uterus), Prostate, Testes, Ovaries	Red	Survival, reproduction pleasure	**Positive:** Feeling safe & connected, Enjoying pleasure & sexuality **Negative:** Feeling unsafe or not enough, Hate the body & self, Non-sexual, weak non-existent orgasms	I am safe, I am enough, I am orgasmic, I love life, pleasure, & sexuality	LAM
SECOND: Sacral	Belly, Hips, Lower back, Womb, Spleen, Liver, Pancreas	Orange	Express emotions, Healing, Balance & harmonize energy & functions of body	**Positive:** Balance & flow, Flexibility, Physical health & strength **Negative:** Playing victim, Feeling stuck, Numb, Rigid	I am in the flow, I am in tune with myself & others, I am confident	VAM
THIRD: Solar Plexus	Solar plexus, Digestive System, Lower & middle spine, Adrenals	Yellow	Center of identity, Power center, Determination & Will power	**Positive:** Independence, Self-sufficiency, Leadership **Negative:** Powerless, Afraid, Co-dependent	I know who I am, I am powerful, I am free	RAM
FOURTH: Heart Center	Chest, Arms & hands, Lungs, Heart, Circulatory System, Thymus	Green	Love & intimacy, Bridges the upper & lower chakras, Unity with life	**Positive:** Love, Compassion, Ability to merge, Forgiveness **Negative:** Depression, Isolation, Worthlessness, Jealousy	I love & am lovable, I am vulnerable & open, I am one with all that is	YAM
FIFTH: Throat Center	Throat & neck, Vocal cords, Ears, Mouth, Thyroid	Blue	To communicate truth	**Positive:** Creativity, Integrity, Truthfulness **Negative:** Dishonesty, Manipulation, Repression	I express my truth, I create with love	HAM
SIXTH: 3rd Eye Center	3rd Eye (middle of forehead), Brain, Eyes, Nose, Pituitary	Violet	Intuition, Inner wisdom	**Positive:** Inspiration, Seeing the whole picture, Inner-directed **Negative:** Directionless, Meaninglessness	I follow my inner guidance	AÏM (AA–EE–MM)
SEVENTH: Crown Center	Crown of the head, Cerebral cortex, Pineal gland	Golden White Light	To connect to divinity	**Positive:** Oneness with all that is, Enlightenment **Negative:** Fear of going crazy, Despair	I am one with all that is, Divinity is in me as me through me	OM

Adapted from material found in *The Sevenfold Journey* by Anodea Judith and Selene Vega and in *Everyday Ecstasy* by Margot Anand

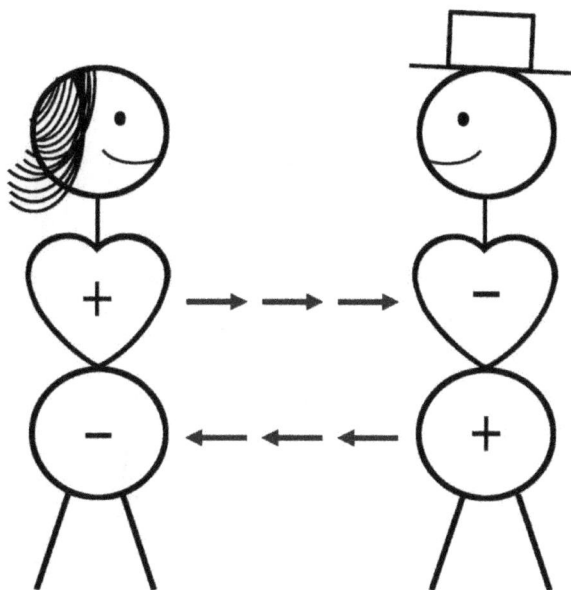

Positive & Negative Energy Poles
of Women & Men

Adapted from *Tantric Orgasm for Women* by Diane Richardson

The PLISSIT Model

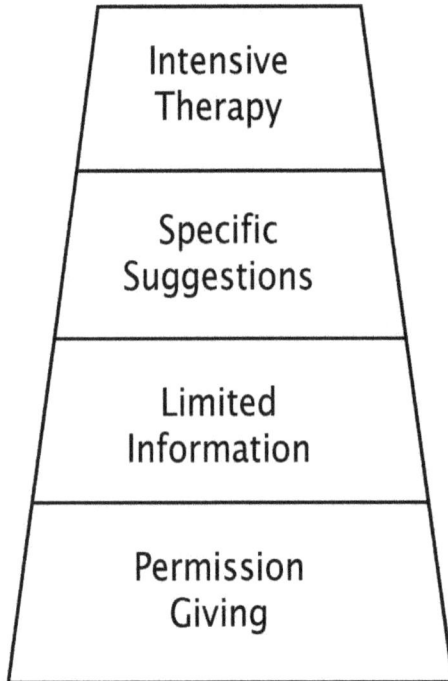

Intensive
Therapy

Specific
Suggestions

Limited
Information

Permission
Giving

This model was created by Jack Annon

Stress

↓

Choice

↙   ↘

Defend   # Open Up

Stay closed   Be
through   Vulnerable

↓   ↓

Defenses   Take
of   Risks
Fight
Flight   ↓
Adapt
Results
↓   **in**
Growth
Results in
maintaning
Status
Quo

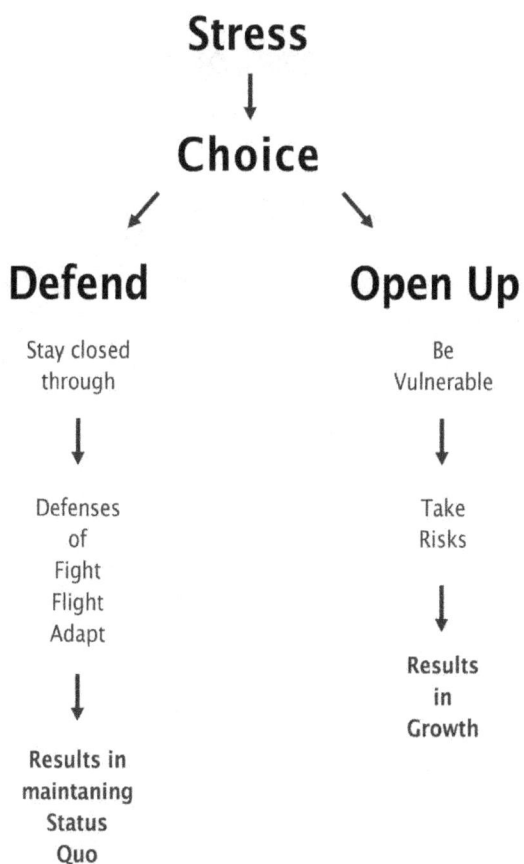

Adapted from Gay and Kathlyn Hendricks workshops

The Wheel of Life

Where is your life out of balance?

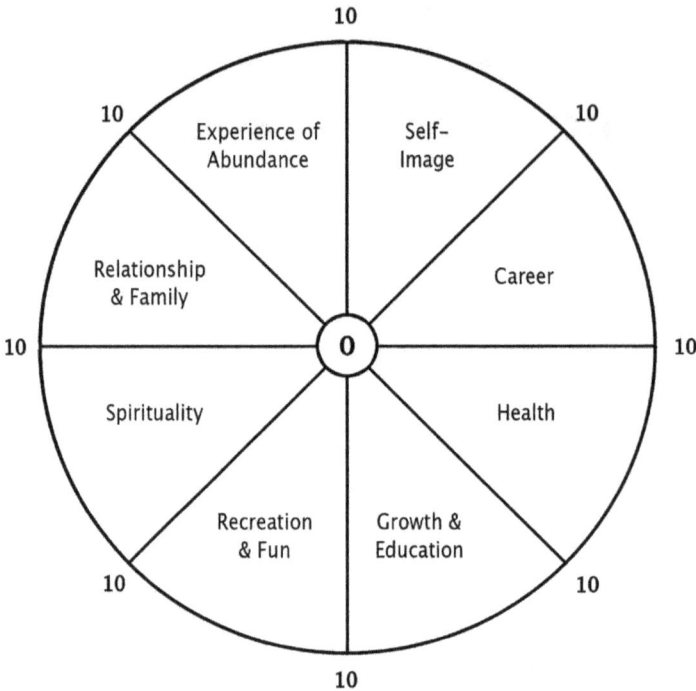

On a scale of 1–10, rate the current level that you
honestly feel you are participating in your life in each area.
Try not to judge where you are — this is only about awareness!
Remember that wherever you are is just fine!

Extended Sexual Response Cycle in Men and Women

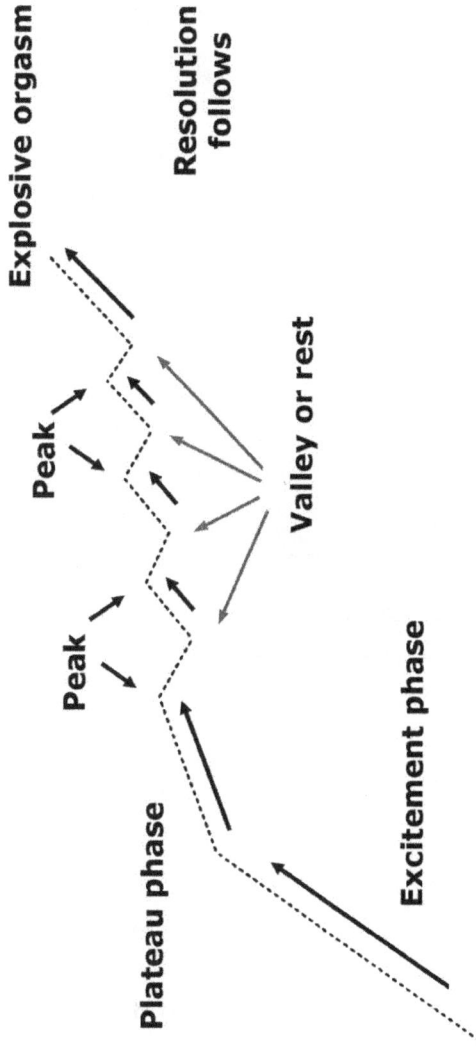

Explosive orgasm

Resolution follows

Peak

Peak

Valley or rest

Plateau phase

Excitement phase

Source: *The Everything Great Sex Book* by Suzie Heumann and Susan Campbell, p. 83

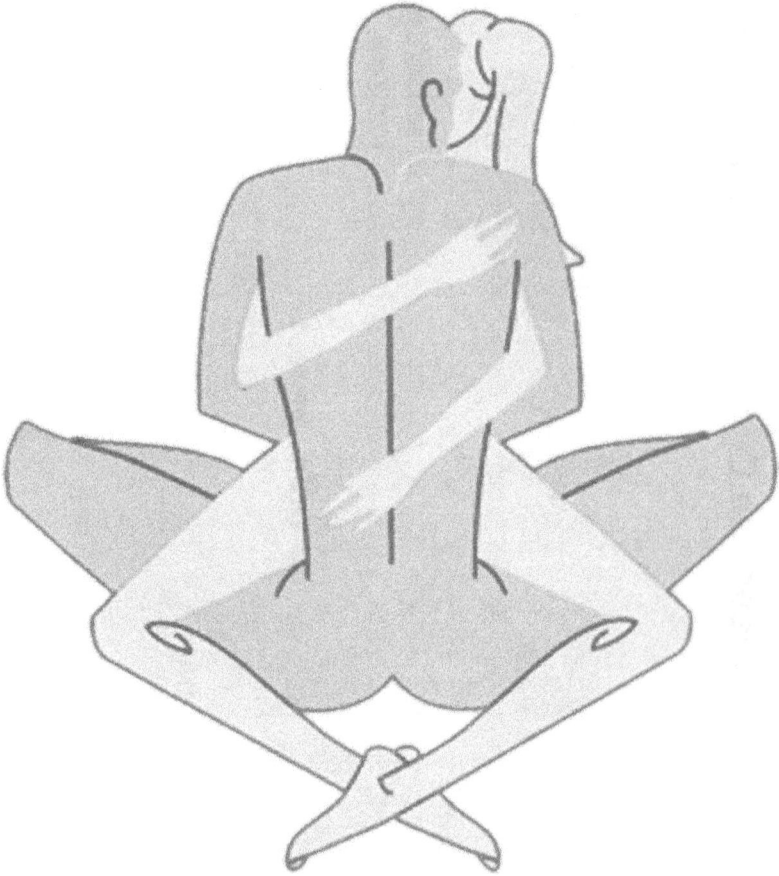

The Yab Yum Position

Acknowledgements

My friend Bill has been a primary source of inspiration, motivation, vision and empowerment for self-publishing this book. Without him, I would not have realized this dream. Thank you, Bill, from the bottom of my heart. I also thank Melanie, Bill's wife, for her friendship and wonderful support. I love how you see the best in me, Melanie, and celebrate it. Thank you!

My teachers, Margot Anand, and Steve & Lokita Carter have been an amazing source of growth that I never dreamed possible. Through their loving, dedicated, wise, sensitive direction and support, I have grown more deeply than I ever have in my life. I now carry with me love, joy, wisdom and peace that I will have forever. I also have an ability to be intimate with myself and others that is a priceless treasure. I feel free of the codependency that has bound me to live life through others instead of myself. I have so much joy and gratitude, and yes, Margot and Steve & Lokita, I now live ecstatically! Thank you!

Thank you, too, for the wonderful community of tantra practitioners that have taught me how to be vulnerable and to stay in my power at the same time. Thank you especially for the wonderful conscious men who have taught me about my inner and outer beauty and how special it is to be a woman. Thank you to one very special man, my life partner, Glenn. You see me and love all of me. Thank Goddess, I have found you.

Thank you to my women friends who have heard it all and seen me through the ups and downs of my life. Thank you especially for Lizi, an amazing tantrika who has held the vision of what sacred sexuality is and how important it is to live consciously, lovingly, passionately and to be in the sacred mystery of the present moment.

Thank you to the Universal Source of All That is. I am manifesting my dreams, thanks to YOU. Namaste!

www.ingramcontent.com/pod-product-compliance
Lightning Source LLC
LaVergne TN
LVHW011224080426
835509LV00005B/314